Monetary Union in the Gulf

At a time of momentous shifts in the balance of world economic forces epitomized by the current oil price boom, the weakening US dollar and the global credit crunch, the meteoric rise of the Arabian Peninsula cannot be understated. Neither, therefore, can their planned monetary union. As key suppliers of the world's oil and gas the Gulf states have accumulated vast wealth: taken together their sovereign wealth funds are by far the world's largest and the influence of these funds is becoming increasingly apparent. This book provides a thorough analysis of the scheduled 2010 monetary union. Its findings are based on both primary research and a detailed empirical analysis of the region's economies spanning 1980–2006. It assesses the region against optimal currency area criteria, the European criteria, highlights outstanding preparations and considers the underlying economic and political factors that may aid or indeed delay the launch date. Critically this book argues that the present dollar-peg exchange rate regimes are no longer optimal. The future Gulf dinar is likely to seek a more independent path. The ramifications of this – a potential Islamic anchor currency and an alternative oil-invoicing currency – are also considered in some detail.

Emilie J. Rutledge is Assistant Professor of Economics at the United Arab Emirates National University. She regularly contributes articles and opinion pieces on GCC economic issues to the regional press. Previously she worked as an economist at the Gulf Research Center, a Dubai-based think tank.

Emilie J. Rutledge's new book, *Monetary Union in the Gulf: prospects for a single currency in the Arabian Peninsula* is the first systematic, book-length treatment of the case for and against monetary union among the members of the Gulf Cooperation Council. It redefines the field of exchange rate economics for the Gulf states and raises the debate to a new and higher level. The book is as excellent as it is timely. Each of the GCC members is engaged in an evaluation of the merits and demerits of the bilateral US dollar pegs that have been the dominant exchange rate regime of the region. Dr Rutledge presents the relevant economic theories clearly and marshals the empirical evidence convincingly. Her familiarity with and deep understanding of the region permit her to address not only the technical, financial and economic issues but also the political economy drivers of the choice of currency regime. **This book is destined to become a classic and is required reading for all those interested in exchange rate issues in resource-based economies, a category that is rather wider than the GCC.**

Willem H. Buiter (*Professor of European Political Economy, European Institute, London School of Economics and Political Science, UK*)

This book comes at a crucial and timely moment. Changes in the balance of global economic power, and the huge wealth being accumulated by Gulf states, mean that an effective Gulf Monetary Union would have far-reaching effects on the global economy. Rutledge's careful analysis of the prospects and requirements is exactly what is needed.

Professor Timothy Niblock (*Institute of Arabic and Islamic Studies, Exeter University, UK*)

Durham modern Middle East and Islamic world series

Series Editor: Anoushiravan Ehteshami

University of Durham

1. **Economic Development in Saudi Arabia**
   Rodney Wilson, with Abdullah Al-Salamah, Monica Malik and Ahmed Al-Rajhi

2. **Islam Encountering Globalisation**
   Edited by Ali Mohammadi

3. **China's Relations with Arabia and the Gulf, 1949–1999**
   Mohamed Bin Huwaidin

4. **Good Governance in the Middle East Oil Monarchies**
   Edited by Tom Pierre Najem and Martin Hetherington

5. **The Middle East's Relations with Asia and Russia**
   Edited by Hannah Carter and Anoushiravan Ehteshami

6. **Israeli Politics and the Middle East Peace Process, 1988–2002**
   Hassan A. Barari

7. **The Communist Movement in the Arab World**
   Tareq Y. Ismael

8. **Oman – The Islamic Democratic Tradition**
   Hussein Ghubash

9. **The Secret Israeli–Palestinian Negotiations in Oslo**
   Their success and why the process ultimately failed
   Sven Behrendt

10. **Globalization and Geopolitics in the Middle East**
    Old games, new rules
    Anoushiravan Ehteshami

Monetary Union in the Gulf

Prospects for a single currency in the Arabian Peninsula

Emilie J. Rutledge

Routledge
Taylor & Francis Group
LONDON AND NEW YORK

First published 2009
by Routledge
2 Park Square, Milton Park, Abingdon, Oxon OX14 4RN

Simultaneously published in the USA and Canada
by Routledge
270 Madison Ave, New York, NY 10016

Routledge is an imprint of the Taylor & Francis Group, an informa business

Typeset in Times by Wearset Ltd, Boldon, Tyne and Wear
Printed and bound in Great Britain by MPG Books Ltd, Bodmin

British Library Cataloguing in Publication Data
A catalogue record for this book is available from the British Library

Library of Congress Cataloging in Publication Data
Rutledge, Emilie J., 1975–
Monetary union in the Gulf: prospects for a single currency in the Arabian Peninsula/Emilie J. Rutledge.
p. cm. – (Durham modern Middle East and Islamic world series; 13)
Includes bibliographical references and index.
1. Monetary unions–Persian Gulf States. I. Title.
HG1212.R88 2008
332.4'5660953–dc22 2008009227

ISBN10: 0-415-45942-7 (hbk)
ISBN10: 0-203-89167-8 (ebk)

ISBN13: 978-0-415-45942-6 (hbk)
ISBN13: 978-0-203-89167-4 (ebk)

Contents

Figures

Tables

Foreword

The subject of Gulf Cooperation Council (GCC) monetary union has been much in the news in recent years, not least because having a target for the introduction of a single currency by 2010 looked extremely ambitious, if not unrealizable, despite the benefits that this might bring in terms of savings on transactions costs and the increased integration of Gulf capital markets. Oman's decision to opt out of the proposed monetary union and Kuwait's abandonment of the US dollar peg for its currency illustrated the fragility of the monetary union project and the difficulty of moving to closer integration even among countries with a common language, similar cultures and the same challenges of economic diversification and job creation for local citizens.

It is important to see beyond current business media headlines and have a deeper perspective of the underlying issues influencing policy choices. This is the value of this study by Dr Emilie Rutledge, the first exhaustive investigation of the challenges of GCC monetary union. As is fitting in any solid piece of academic research, relevant theories are examined, notably optimal currency area theory, originally applied to resource rich-Canada, but arguably also of relevance to the resource rich GCC. The classic preconditions for an optimal currency area do not appear to be met in the GCC however, as much stress was placed on factor mobility involving labour and capital, as well as a high proportion of intra-regional rather than extra-regional trade.

A critical feature of the Mundell model for an optimal currency area is the assumption that for monetary union to succeed participants should have similar Phillips curves, implying a common trade-off between unemployment and inflation. The original negative relationship has long broken down in Europe and North America, and in the GCC unemployment data is unreliable and not very meaningful as the problem of youth unemployment is structural rather than cyclical and caused more by supply than demand factors rendering monetary policy useless. Yet in the GCC this means that there are less likely to be losses from a pooling of monetary sovereignty regardless of differences in labour market conditions between member states, as short-term monetary expansions or loosening of monetary policy will not by itself increase employment opportunities for local nationals.

As the currencies of Saudi Arabia, Bahrain, Qatar and the UAE have long been pegged to the US dollar and there are no restrictions on financial transfers, the advantages and disadvantages of free capital mobility have already been realized. Monetary union will therefore arguably make little difference, and as in the Eurozone, separate national or even sub-national financial markets will continue to exist reflecting legal and regulatory differences. For portfolio investors there are likely to be gains from a single currency, however, as apart from in Saudi Arabia designing a diverse equity portfolio to reduce risk is problematic and even market risk is reduced by having multiple market exposure. At present there are no impairments to having a GCC-wide portfolio, and such funds already exist, but there are currency transaction costs which would be eliminated, and denomination in a common currency across markets facilitates stock performance comparisons.

Rutledge provides a detailed picture of the GCC economies over the period 1980–2006 and utilizes this to put forward a detailed cost/benefit analysis of the proposed GCC monetary union. Progress to date and outstanding preparations are also set out in considerable detail. She considers the need for institutional reform and fiscal convergence to be particularly important, terming this as the *European criteria*, and furthermore contends that for the GCC, *indirect benefits* (those occurring as a result of the process of forming a single currency) may bring more immediate benefits than do the *direct benefits* arising of the monetary union itself.

Semi-structured interviews and a region-wide business survey were carried out to ascertain the opinions of leading central bankers, policymakers and the business community regarding on the proposed monetary union. What is worth mentioning is that almost none stressed the gains from increased price transparency with a common currency, a factor which has proved of major significance in the Eurozone and which could also be important in the GCC given the extent of intra-regional travel by local nationals. Increased awareness by Saudi visitors of just how expensive Dubai actually is, for example, might result in some curtailment of price increases, if not reductions.

There have been press articles and editorials in the Gulf press blaming the currency peg with the US dollar for the surge in domestic inflation, with exchange rate policy becoming subject to increasing debate given the US dollars depreciation, most notably against the euro and sterling, in which a significant proportion of GCC imports are denominated. Yet abandonment of the dollar peg is unlikely in the near future, not least because oil, gas and petrochemical exports from the GCC are dollar denominated and the political relationship with the United States is valued by GCC governments in strategic terms, not least for security reasons. Furthermore, although an increasingly significant proportion of GCC imports originate in Asia, these are also US dollar denominated and they have increased relatively to euro-denominated imports. GCC exchange rate policies are therefore unlikely to change, unless Asian currencies are meaningfully uncoupled from the US dollar and appreciate significantly. The abandonment of oil price denomination in US dollars is also likely to be a precondition for exchange rate policy change, not least because even the Kuwait basket is US dollar heavy.

In the longer term such external changes are likely however, the issue being whether the GCC states have any strategy to deal with international currency crises. As clearly they don't, the value of Rutledge's study is that it draws attention to exchange rate issues and encourages debate. Monetary union by 2010 is certainly not realizable, but the currency debate in the GCC has only just begun and in the longer term the members will inevitably be currency price makers, not takers, with a new GCC currency perhaps the denominator for energy pricing of choice.

Professor Rodney Wilson
Durham University, UK

Acknowledgements

I would like to express my sincere thanks and gratitude to the following individuals and institutions for the support and assistance they provided. First and foremost I would like to thank the following individuals at Durham University, where the idea for this book was first hatched, in particular Professor Rodney Wilson, Professor Anoush Ehteshami and Dr Mehmet Asutay. I also appreciate the encouragement and advice given to me by Professor Timothy Niblock of Exeter University. I would like to thank the Economic and Social Research Council for the financial assistance they provided which enabled me to undertake primary research in the region. Turning to the Arabian Gulf, I'm particularly indebted to the Chairman of the Dubai-based Gulf Research Center, Sheikh Abdulaziz Sager, for his valuable insights and support. Finally, I would like to thank my colleagues at the UAE University, in particular the Secretary General Dr Fatima Al-Shamsi and Professor Abdulrazak Al-Faris, for providing me with numerous excellent contacts across the region.

Abbreviations

/b	per barrel of oil
AMF	Arab Monetary Fund
BRIC	Brazil, Russia, India and China
CPI	consumer price inflation
Cu. Ft/d	cubic feet per day
EMI	European Monetary Institute
EMU	European Monetary Union
ESCWA	Economic and Social Commission for Western Asia
EU	European Union
FDI	foreign direct investment
FTA	free trade agreement
FTZ	free trade zone
GCC	Gulf Cooperation Council
GDP	gross domestic product
IEA	International Energy Agency
IFS	International Financial Statistics
ILO	International Labour Organisation
IMF	International Monetary Fund
IOC	International Oil Company
IPO	initial public offering
KSA	(Kingdom of) Saudi Arabia
mbpd	million barrels per day
MENA	Middle East and North Africa
MU	monetary union
OCA	optimal currency area
OPEC	Organization of the Petroleum Exporting Countries
PPP	purchasing power parity
SAMA	Saudi Arabian Monetary Agency
SGP	Stability and Growth Pact
SME	small and medium sized enterprise
TIR	trade intensity ratio
UAE	United Arab Emirates
UN	United Nations

UNCTAD	United Nations Conference on Trade and Development
UNDP	United Nations Development Program
US	United States (of America)
WDI	world development indicator
WTO	World Trade Organization

1 Introduction

In 1980 six states on the Arabian Peninsula (Bahrain, Kuwait, Oman, Qatar, Saudi Arabia and the United Arab Emirates) formed the Gulf Cooperation Council (GCC). For 20 years the impact of this event barely registered on the world's media antennae. But since the beginning of the twenty-first century these states have been making the headlines with increasing frequency and not only because of their geographic proximity to Iraq and Iran or their position as the world's key supplier of oil and gas. A string of high-profile overseas acquisitions – including P&O and Madame Tussaud's – and the region's unprecedented construction boom have also contributed to a worldwide perception that some kind of tectonic shift is taking place in the world's economic and strategic geography. And while Western observers look on with a mixture of admiration, disdainful hauteur and not a little anxiety, such 'excesses' as the Emirate of Dubai's man-made palm tree-shaped islands, the world's tallest building and ski-slopes in the desert, nevertheless add further conviction to the view that 'something of massive proportions' is happening in the Arabian Peninsula.

It is therefore in this context that the growing role of the Gulf's political organization – the GCC, and, in particular, its major 'project' the adoption of a single currency, must be understood and evaluated. Indeed, one could go further. At a time of momentous shifts in the balance of world economic forces epitomized by the precipitate fall in the US dollar and the global credit crunch; the meteoric rise of the Arabian Peninsula to which we have alluded cannot be understated. The pivotal position GCC sovereign currencies have vis-à-vis the value of the US dollar is becoming increasingly apparent.

Five of the six GCC states have maintained dollar pegs for most of this book's period of study: 1980–2006; and the dollar is undoubtedly a key component of Kuwait's basket peg. Their oil is invoiced in dollars and most of their surplus 'petrodollar' revenues have – until recently at least – been recycled back into US government-issued securities. However, when the *Gulf dinar*, as we shall term it, comes into existence, the consequences may be of critical importance to both the US and world economies. Not only would a Gulf dinar undoubtedly become the Middle East's and the Islamic world's most significant currency as well as the world's second most important common currency, it may also present the GCC states with an opportune moment to de-peg from the dollar.

Reprising the fundamental economic underpinning of that 'tectonic shift' in the Arabian Peninsula's geo-strategic position, let us remind ourselves of a few critical facts: The states comprising the GCC currently supply 23 per cent of the world's crude oil – a figure which is set to increase considerably in the coming decades. They also sit on 40 per cent of the world's proven oil reserves and nearly a quarter of the world's proven gas reserves. Unlike previous oil booms, these states are seemingly no longer content to simply export crude oil and recycle all of their windfall earnings back into the oil-importing industrialized economies. Instead they are using some of this surplus capital to expand their own refining and petrochemical capacities, enabling them to retain more of the 'value-added' value that has traditionally been generated and collected by Western oil and petrochemical companies. The GCC is also forging new strategic alliances with Asia by investing billions of dollars in Chinese and Indian refineries and petrochemical plants – many are being designed specifically to handle Gulf crudes.

The second critical fact is the huge financial wealth (and possibly with it influence) amassed by the region's governments. With the huge increase in oil prices that has occurred since the beginning of the decade, the bloc's current account surpluses are growing at a rate similar to that of the US's current account deficit and are comparable in size to China's huge surplus. Between 2002 and 2006 the GCC amassed some $558 billion in net foreign assets and their stock of foreign assets is now estimated to be worth $1.6 trillion (IIF 2007). In 2007 their sovereign wealth funds bought significant stakes in a wide range of international banks and private equity firms including HSBC, Standard Chartered and the Carlyle Group. When the UAE's Abu Dhabi Investment Authority – rumoured to manage $900 billion worth of government funds – purchased a 4.9 per cent stake in Citibank for $7.5 billion, it marked the clearest sign yet that the Arabian Peninsula states are no longer content to place all of their surplus capital into US government securities. The implication of this for the dollar's dominant position and its role as the de facto oil-invoicing currency remains to be seen.

This book is intended to give an account of the GCC's longstanding goal of becoming a monetary union (MU). It will chart the history and key developments to date and consider its appropriateness, using both the optimal currency area (OCA) benchmark and more recent criteria drawing upon the European Monetary Union (EMU) experience – the latter we term the *European criteria*. It will look at the outstanding prerequisites and necessary policy reforms, arguing that political determination and commitment, rather than purely economic factors are slowing down the process. It will also assess the longer term prospects: will MU bring net benefits for all participating states? Is it conceivable that one day the Gulf dinar will be viewed a viable anchor currency for the Middle East or even the Islamic world and even possibly be used to invoice the region's oil sales? As we have already indicated, these are not just issues of interest to economists specializing in the Middle East, but also major questions of political and geo-strategic importance as we move into the second decade of the twenty-first century.

The present conjuncture

Although five of the six GCC states still officially plan to adopt a common currency by 1 January 2010 (Oman surprised many by unilaterally opting out in December 2006), the launch date may well end up being postponed for a number of years. This is because many of the prerequisite policy reforms, such as establishing a fully functioning common market, setting up a GCC central bank and meeting a set of fiscal and monetary convergence criteria, have yet to take place. However, the region's MU plans are likely to remain on the agenda, in part because of the perceived economic benefits but also because it represents the culmination of a longstanding ambition for deeper regional integration. Nevertheless, it must be acknowledged that in reality, an MU will never be entered into for economic reasons alone. Ultimately any decision will be borne out of political considerations and only achieved with concerted political will.

Arguably the GCC countries are now in an ideal fiscal position to move ahead with economic reform including the MU project as they have ample funds to soften any transitional costs. High oil prices since 2002 have resulted in a region-wide economic boom which has been the most pronounced throughout the period covered in this study (1980–2006). As an indicator of the huge increase in the Gulf's income during the last few years, in 2006 their collective current account surplus of $176 billion rivalled that of China's. All the more impressive when one considers the fact that the GCC has a population of just 35 million compared to China's 1.3 billion. Many energy analysts predict that current oil prices and levels of demand will be in place for a number of years to come; some even believe a 'price paradigm shift' has now taken place. A 2007 International Energy Agency report projected that global oil demand would increase by 2.2 per cent annually, climbing from 86.1 million barrels per day (mbpd) to reach 95.8mbpd by 2012.

Nevertheless, the 'feel-good factor' brought on by these huge oil price windfalls, seems if anything, to have reduced the urgency with which the MU project is being pursued. Indeed, it is worth noting that the Gulf's most unambiguous commitment to MU and regional economic integration – the signing of the new GCC Economic Agreement – was taken in 2001, at the tail-end of a protracted period of low oil prices, coupled with stagnating growth rates and, in many cases, declining per capita incomes. It would seem that the region's vast new wealth might be encouraging the view – at least among some members – that hydrocarbons alone can float their citizens into an endless future of economic wellbeing, avoiding the difficult economic and political reforms which are part and parcel of the MU project, not least the devolution of hitherto jealously guarded sovereign powers to supranational GCC institutions and the need for greater fiscal discipline and budget accountability.

But no matter how well-endowed with hydrocarbon resources, those resources are nevertheless finite and depleting and while there may be some conjunctural nonchalance about the current state of affairs there are still many statesmen, economists and opinion formers in the Gulf who recognize that economic diversification must remain an ultimate policy objective and that MU will be one of the essential factors in broadening the GCC's economic base.

The choice of model

Naturally, as with any such major policy endeavour, opinions on the economic utility of a GCC MU are mixed. On the one hand, it has been argued that there will be few advantages, as member economies already have stable exchange rates vis-à-vis one another and therefore, will not benefit substantially from conventional advantages of MU such as the elimination of exchange rate risk. As intra-GCC trade is considered low, a reduction in transaction costs will likewise, not provide significant gains. Jadresic (2002) for instance, concluded that 'the benefits do not seem too large . . . neither do the costs'.

On the other hand, and as this book will point out, there are likely to be a range of advantages, both conventional MU ones and associated ones. Many of the latter can be characterized as indirect outcomes. We view these as significant *associated advantages* as they will benefit the general polity and society of the Gulf states (for example the implicit need for more transparency and budget accountability will enhance private sector confidence, the need for greater fiscal discipline should foster more balanced and sustainable growth). At the same time, we also acknowledge that those who benefit from the opaque status quo, may conceivably view what we term 'associated advantages' as not being advantageous and rather as 'costs' or 'obstacles'.

It should also be stated from the outset that the magnitude of any costs or benefits arising from a GCC MU will depend not only on a range of variables including the degree to which the Gulf states meet structural criteria and the degree of preparations made in the lead-up to MU but also on what type of MU the bloc decides to implement. At one end of the spectrum is the Eurozone, at the other is the Eastern Caribbean Currency Union (ECCU)[1] and the three French franc zones.[2]

Unlike the euro which is a free floating currency, the East Caribbean dollar has maintained a fixed peg to the US dollar since 1976. Eight Caribbean states share this currency and it is managed by a single institution – the East Caribbean Central Bank. The IMF (2007e) defines the ECCU as a 'quasi-currency board arrangement' and credits it with delivering both price and exchange rate stability and fostering a relatively deep and stable financial system. A currency board system is considered to add credibility to a fixed exchange rate regime (De Grauwe 2007).

The French franc zones' common currencies are similar to the East Caribbean dollar in that they also maintain a fixed peg to an anchor currency, in this case the euro, but the nature of the MU is different. Primarily France guarantees convertibility at a fixed rate into euros for these currencies, in return France has representation on the two regional central bank's executive boards and MU members are required to deposit 65 per cent of their exchange reserves with the French central bank (Healy 2003). Having a fully convertible currency is generally considered to increase FDI inflows and encourage private domestic investment (capital retention).

The question of whether a future Gulf dinar would remain loyal to the dollar peg, as alluded to at the outset of this introduction, or opt for an alternative form of exchange rate regime is a subject of enormous speculation in both the regional and international financial press. In a similar vein to the ambiguity that surrounds the MU project in general, GCC government officials and central bank governors have often given mixed signals on what the future regime is likely to be. Currently, the consensus view is that the new currency would initially stick with the status quo and alternatives such as a trade-weighted peg or a some form of free float would be considered at a later date.

Undoubtedly the launch of the euro in 1999, and its subsequent success, rekindled the GCC's interest in proceeding with their own MU plans. Indeed, at the 2001 GCC summit, at which members set out a clear timetable for achieving MU by 2010, King Abdullah of Saudi Arabia stated that the EMU was the 'model to follow' (Al-Saud 2002). The European Central Bank (ECB) has provided direct assistance to the GCC by providing a 'draft monetary agreement' for the GCC MU (Ameen 2006a). The ECB has also run a series of workshops with the GCC Secretariat's MU technical committee and the Payment Systems Committee while the former head of the IMF, Rodrigo Rato, has suggested that on their path towards a single currency the GCC should learn from European institutions such as Eurostat – a supranational data-gathering and statistical agency that helped assess EMU convergence prior to the euro's launch (Al-Mansouri and Dziobek 2006). Nevertheless, there may be features of EMU which are in some instances inappropriate and in others highly challenging for the Gulf states, as we shall see later in this book.

Regional monetary precedents and problems

There are some regional precedents to the planned GCC MU, which, in a similar vein to the ECCU and French franc zones, have a link to former colonial rule. Since the 1950s, with the exception of Saudi Arabia, which has had its own currency since Ottoman times, all of the present-day GCC states once used a common currency, the Indian rupee, reflecting the dominant role of Britain's Indian Empire in the Arabian Peninsula. Between 1959 and 1966 these states actually used their own distinct common currency known as the Gulf rupee, but pegged to the Indian currency.[3] However, after gaining independence in 1961, Kuwait replaced this with its own sovereign currency, the Kuwaiti dinar.

In the early 1960s several Gulf states sought to establish an independent MU. This culminated in 1965 with the signing of the Arabian Gulf Currency Agreement by Abu Dhabi, Bahrain, Dubai and Qatar. Under this agreement an MU was to be formed and a common currency would be introduced for general circulation. However, differences emerged during the implementation process and as a consequence, Qatar and Dubai decided to form their own MU and signed the Qatar–Dubai Currency Agreement in March 1966 (Symes 1997). The agreement provided for the introduction of a common currency and the establishment of a currency board to manage it.

In June 1966, India devalued its own currency and the Gulf rupee declined with it (Johri and Miller 2002). Most Gulf states did not feel a devaluation was appropriate for their economies and sought alternatives. During the transition away from the Gulf rupee all the Gulf states briefly used the Saudi riyal but eventually Qatar and most of the Emirates that now comprise the UAE agreed to start using their own recently agreed upon single currency, the Qatar and Dubai riyal. However, the Emirate of Abu Dhabi opted for the currency of the newly independent Bahrain, the Bahraini dinar. This left only Oman using the Gulf rupee and it continued to do so until 1970 when its own sovereign currency, the Omani rial, was introduced. The Qatar and Dubai riyal continued to circulate even after Qatar gained independence in 1971 and Dubai, also gaining independence, became a member of the UAE in the same year. It was not in fact until 1973 that the riyal ceased to be legal tender. It is also worth bearing in mind that the seven Emirates of the UAE, whose economies were, and are, by no means homogenous, all adopted the Emirati dirham without any documented monetary complications.

By the mid-1970s, with turbulent political, economic and military events rocking the whole Middle East, there was a renewed interest in MU among the Gulf states. In 1975, Kuwait's Central Bank commissioned Professor Robert Mundell – who established the foundations of the OCA theory – to assess the region's suitability for MU; at this time the plan was to include *only four* of what are now the six GCC states – Bahrain, Kuwait, Qatar and the UAE (Al-Hajji 1999). Nevertheless, soon after its formation in 1981, the GCC adopted the wide-ranging Unified Economic Agreement (GCC Secretariat General 1981) which set out a framework for full economic integration and stated that *all six* states would 'endeavor to establish a joint currency'.

The 2001 Economic Agreement and after

A shared culture, language, religion and resource dependence should theoretically make the relinquishing of sovereign currencies less politically contentious and emotive than was the case in the Eurozone countries prior to 1999. Yet, apart from the GCC states signing a free trade agreement (FTA) in 1983, there was little tangible progress until the December 2001 GCC summit where leaders re-energized their economic integration efforts. At the summit of 2001 a revised economic agreement was signed and although broadly based on the original 1981 economic agreement, the language was more specific. For instance, Article Four stipulated that all members would work towards a specific timetable in order to prepare for monetary unification (GCC Secretariat General 2001).

The 2001 Economic Agreement listed specific steps that would need to be taken in order to establish a GCC MU. They included fostering a high level of harmonization in all economic policy areas, particularly fiscal and monetary policy and setting economic convergence criteria related to monetary and fiscal stability. It was agreed that a customs union be established as soon as possible, convergence targets set in 2005, a common market completed by 2007 and for a GCC single currency to be launched by 2010 (GCC Secretariat General 2001).

The GCC Secretariat is the main supranational institution in the Gulf and is located in Saudi Arabia with a staff of several hundred. In 2002 the GCC Supreme Council set up a Monetary Unit at the Secretariat, however its role and influence are debatable – to date it has published no research papers or policy recommendations on the proposed MU which are in the public domain. It remains the case that most (provisional) decisions are made by the bloc's respective central bank governors who meet twice a year and report to the GCC Committee for Financial and Economic Cooperation.

Yet all binding decision making powers ultimately rest with the region's rulers. For instance in 2006, the UAE Central Bank governor, Sultan Al-Suwaidi, said that central bankers had reached agreement on several issues and passed these onto the Committee for Financial and Economic Cooperation. These issues included 'agreement on the framework of the proposed common monetary authority, or the GCC's central bank, and its relationship with the individual central banks, as well as payment systems and the suggested reserves'. Al-Suwaidi, added that the 'draft monetary agreement [was] based on the draft agreement that was provided by the European Central Bank' (Ameen 2006a). Yet to date, none of these decisions appears to have been officially endorsed and the GCC central bank is yet to be established.

The GCC agreed to officially peg their respective currencies to the dollar by 2003 in order to stabilize bilateral exchange rates in the lead-up to MU. For most this was essentially a cost-free move as they already had de facto pegs to the dollar, Kuwait alone had to modify its exchange rate regime from a basket peg but retained a band of adjustment of ±3.5 per cent.

In 2003, in what was considered a major achievement towards integration, the GCC began the first phase of setting up a customs union that harmonized external tariffs to five per cent and removed intra-regional ones. Yet the final stage of the customs union, scheduled for the end of 2005, has been complicated by the discord arising from Bahrain's decision (later followed by Oman) to 'go it alone' and sign a bilateral FTA with the US. It was agreed at the 2005 GCC summit that the interim period for the customs union would be extended until the end of 2007.

It was widely anticipated that the GCC would formally adopt a set of convergence criteria at the 2005 summit, not least because the bloc's central bank governors had reportedly agreed on the style of convergence criteria (along the lines of Europe's Maastricht criteria), but at the summit it was agreed that finance ministers needed more time to consider them. Yet according to officials at the GCC Monetary Union Unit ministers have since agreed upon a set of monetary and fiscal convergence criteria.

However, at the 2005 GCC summit leaders did agree to exempt most goods from tariffs and to allow Gulf nationals to conduct commercial activities across the bloc, most notably giving full access to one another's bourses. Gulf nationals do not need passports to travel between GCC states and they are also allowed to own property and many types of business in neighbouring states. As this book goes to press, the GCC Secretariat announced on 1 January 2008 that a GCC common market had come into being. However, the Secretariat acknowledged that the common market is far from complete given that it may take many months, if not longer, to negotiate the harmonization of legislation across the bloc.

Although little progress on the path to MU has been made and scepticism in the regional press has grown, up until 2006, there had been no actual setbacks. This changed in 2006 when Oman opted out altogether. Although an MU without Oman is perfectly feasible economically speaking, it nevertheless dealt a political and psychological blow. The Omani government cited the general lack of progress that had thus far been made towards the GCC MU for its decision, but we contend that the growing controversy surrounding the utility of pegging to a weakening dollar and the divergence of opinions on the optimal future exchange rate policy for the future single currency is likely to have been another key factor. While Oman (and probably Bahrain) see advantages in a weak currency (as it makes their non-oil manufactured goods more internationally competitive), Kuwait clearly does not.

The second setback was Kuwait's decision in May 2007 to revert to its pre-2003 exchange rate regime, citing the need to tackle 'imported inflation' through a gradual currency revaluation. This move jeopardized one of the few monetary convergence areas the GCC had been meeting – stable bilateral exchange rates. While the dollar component of Kuwait's basket peg is thought to be substantial, the Kuwaiti dinar will inevitably fluctuate more now vis-à-vis the other currencies (in the five months following this move the Kuwaiti dinar had appreciated by five per cent against the dollar).

The third setback came in September 2007 when Saudi Arabia's central bank governor, Hamad Al-Sayyari, let it be known that GCC central banks had agreed to deal with their respective inflation problems separately (Augustine 2007a). The UAE central bank governor added further uncertainty by warning that the 2010 launch date may need to be put back to 2015. Nevertheless what regional central bankers say and the policy decisions actually taken by GCC leaders are not always in sync. In December 2007, the communiqué of the GCC summit stated that the leaders remained committed to the MU project and the scheduled launch date of 2010 and since September 2007 the monetary policies of the four pegged currencies have not diverged.

While it is our view, given the limited progress to date, that meeting the 2010 deadline now seems ambitious, as regional leaders have invested considerable political capital in the MU project it seems inconceivable that they will abandon it altogether. In addition, the wider geopolitical scene must be taken into consideration. The nations of the Arabian Peninsula lie on a fault line of Middle East tensions – tensions which are unlikely to evaporate in the foreseeable future. In the coming years they may well realize that greater unity of purpose is an essential prerequisite of their survival as both modern and monarchical Islamic states and that MU is a key means to achieving that objective.

Outline of the study

This book has two key objectives: firstly, to assess the appropriateness of MU for the GCC as an economic region and, secondly, to ascertain the costs and benefits, for the bloc as a whole (and where possible on a country-by-country basis). We will also outline some implications and prospects for the Gulf dinar. In addition to primary evidence gathered from a GCC business survey on the subject and the views of regional experts expressed in interviews conducted by the author,[4] this book also uses extensive empirical analysis based on officially published regional datasets – where credible and consistent – and data collated by institutions such as the Arab Monetary Fund (AMF), the International Monetary Fund (IMF), the UN and the World Bank.

This book proceeds as follows: Chapter 2 will begin by providing a macroeconomic overview of the GCC and, where relevant, highlighting the similarities and differences between the member economies. It will focus in detail on the GCC's main economic characteristics, key economic policies and the bloc's performance over the period of study. It will then touch upon some of the challenges facing the region which may well become more pronounced in the coming years and will undoubtedly have a bearing on the MU project; in particular the extent of the GCC's continuing dependence on hydrocarbons and growing national unemployment levels are highlighted.

In Chapter 3 we undertake an assessment of the GCC as a Mundellian 'economic region' and test the bloc against the OCA criteria. According to OCA theory, groups of economies with high levels of intra-regional trade, factor market mobility, economic diversification and business cycle synchronization stand to benefit most from MU. We investigate both quantitatively and qualitatively, the extent to which GCC economies meet the core OCA criteria. This chapter also takes into consideration later empirical research which has concluded that even if a group of economies do not meet all of these criteria prior to forming MU, the process of unification itself may result in these criteria being met.

In Chapter 4 the GCC's progress towards MU is critically assessed. The experience of EMU has illustrated that a number of prerequisite policies and preparations are required in order to establish a stable and sustainable MU; we term these the *European criteria*. In particular, we assess the progress towards establishing a common market, building supranational institutions not least a regional central bank, meeting provisional convergence criteria and preparing the private sector. Finally in this chapter we analyze the GCC leaders' motivation in seeking to establish a single currency and attempt to assess the degree of political commitment to the project – undoubtedly a critical prerequisite for forming an MU.

The potential costs arising from the GCC MU are assessed in Chapter 5, as well as the conventional costs of MU, the analysis will also indicate where additional and at times region specific costs may occur. We consider the cost of losing sovereign control over monetary policy from a dynamic perspective, as well as the potential costs arising from the divergence of macroeconomic policies. The degree to which the imposition of 'Maastricht-style' fiscal rules will be economically costly to these oil dependent economies is also assessed. Finally we examine the perceived 'political costs' to the region's ruling elites, greater fiscal budget accountability and the creation of supranational institutions will inevitably involve the ceding of some sovereign powers.

Chapter 6 considers the likely benefits of MU for the Gulf states. Many of the benefits arising from a single currency are of a microeconomic nature; we analyse the potential efficiency gains arising from reduced transaction costs, exchange rate risk and increased price transparency. The benefit of a single currency in terms of fostering increased trade and capital market growth in the region is also considered. Further associated benefits are also discussed in this chapter, such as the potential for MU to act as a catalyst for economic reform. Preparing for MU will require improvements in fiscal policy management in the region and increasing the transparency of regional budgets as well as building strong independent institutions. Finally the chapter considers the geopolitical gains from achieving full regional economic integration and the degree to which these will act as incentives to spur the process of MU.

Chapter 7 of the book acts as a conclusion to our preceding analysis, summarizing the main findings of our study and providing a preliminary cost–benefit balance sheet of MU for the bloc. It looks at the region-specific importance of the OCA and European criteria in determining how viable and potentially successful a Gulf MU may be. It also considers whether or not all member states will benefit to the same extent from joining the future MU.

Finally, Chapter 8 concentrates on future issues and controversies surrounding the MU, in particular it will focus on the external exchange rate options for the Gulf dinar. At the centre of this question is the debate over the continuing utility of the dollar peg and the possible advantages of a more flexible regime. It will also consider what bearing, if any, the region's commodity dependency has on the prospects of establishing a viable MU. The book closes with a discussion of the geopolitical implications of the Gulf dinar and whether it has the potential to take on a wider regional and even international role.

2 Characteristics of the GCC economies

The Arabian Peninsula states have several distinct economic characteristics which set them apart not only from the rest of the world, but also from the Middle East and North Africa (MENA) region. They have vast oil and gas reserves, the world's largest if measured in barrels of oil per capita, yet unlike many other oil-rich states have very small populations, smaller still if expatriate workers – the majority of the labour force – are factored out. In many respects, their basic infrastructure is comparable to Europe's, education for all Gulf nationals is free including at tertiary level as is access to a universal healthcare system. Most nationals work in the public sector and must be among the world's highest paid civil servants while the private sector is staffed almost exclusively by expatriates and in the unskilled sector predominantly by economic migrants from South and South East Asia. Hence these states are often classified as 'resource rich, labour poor'.

Within MENA the GCC is by far the most active and cohesive economic bloc (it is currently negotiating multilateral FTAs with China, India and the EU); the only comparable, but far less functional grouping, is the Arab Maghreb Union. Over the period of this book's study (1980–2006) the GCC states have together outperformed MENA's 3.6 per cent median annual GDP growth rate, registering 4.1 per cent. More impressively still, in 2006 the GCC's average per capita income was almost quadruple that of MENA's ($23,548 compared to $6,155).

While most institutional economic reports on the MENA pool the GCC states together, at times viewing the bloc as an almost homogeneous entity, our analysis will show that, although there are indeed many commonalities, there are also marked differences. We contend that while all member states face common shocks their responses to them are different. All are now WTO members but there are big differences in terms of economic openness and their ability to attract FDI. Economic diversification away from an overdependence on oil is a shared goal, but a range of alternate strategies are being pursued. Other distinctions include levels of resource endowment, GDP growth, per capita income and inflation rates (see Table 2.1). Some differences have become more pronounced since oil prices began their meteoric rise in 2002 and may well present the MU project with some last minute complications.

This chapter will first outline the dominant role oil plays in all of these

Table 2.1 Selected GCC economic indicators, 2006

	Bahrain	*Kuwait*	*Oman*	*Qatar*	*KSA*	*UAE*	*GCC*
Nominal GDP (US$, bn)	16.07	96.13	35.99	52.72	348.60	168.26	717.78
Nominal GDP growth	18.6%	24.4%	25.1%	30.7%	17.3%	36.4%	23.6%
Real GDP (US$, bn)	9.91	61.22	19.50	27.12	214.56	107.17	439.48
Real GDP growth	7.7%	5.0%	5.9%	8.8%	4.6%	9.7%	6.2%
Population (mn)	0.749	2.967	2.477	0.839	23.691	5.038	35.761
of which are expatriates	*0.284*	*2.16*	*0.666*[a]	*0.620*	*6.409*	*3.805*[a]	*13.944*
GDP per capita (PPP in US$)	23,604	19,909	18,841	33,049	16,744	29,142	23,548
Inflation rate	3.0%	3.0%	3.2%	11.8%	2.3%	10.1%	5.6%
Current account balance (US$, bn)	2.90	41.41	3.03	6.10	95.50	27.35	176.29
Government budget balance (US$, bn)	1.16	30.14	5.69	1.05	70.75	53.46	162.24
Post 2002 net foreign assets (US$, bn)	5.51	112.05	14.46	46.21	302.57	77.13	557.93

Sources: BP (2007); National Bank of Kuwait (2007); IMF (2007a); IMF (2007c).

Notes

a Data for 2005. KSA is the abbreviation for (Kingdom of) Saudi Arabia.

economies – sometimes considered 'black gold', at others a 'resource curse' – and then move on to provide a general overview of the bloc's economic performance. It will look at the structure of GDP, monetary policy issues including inflation rates, trade patterns and investment flows over the period of study. It will then turn to the region's economic challenges, many of which are in some way linked to dependence on oil. The dominant role of the public sector will be discussed as will the highly segmented labour market and growing levels of national unemployment. Diversification strategies, with which we include economic integration and the GCC MU project, will also be touched upon.

Resource riches: the dominance of oil

The GCC sits on over 40 per cent of the world's proven oil reserves and almost a quarter of its natural gas reserves, yet the distribution is by no means equal. Using data for 'proven' reserves and at 2006 production rates Bahrain's oil will be depleted in under a decade and Oman's will also be exhausted in just over two decades (see Table 2.2). While Saudi Arabia has the world's largest reserves, on a per capita basis it equals 11,150 barrels per head, Kuwait has 34,210 barrels per head and the longest reserve 'life expectancy', at current production rates, within the bloc at 103 years. Qatar with an indigenous population of just over 200,000 is not short of oil itself, but has the GCC's largest reserves of natural gas, indeed, they are the third largest globally (see Table 2.2).

While this resource endowment has historically provided the bloc's governments with significant revenues and has enabled them to build a first-class infrastructure, during boom periods it has lead to several bouts of 'Dutch disease': a rapid capital inflow leading to a rise in the price of non-tradables vis-à-vis tradables. During these periods, the domestic non-oil manufacturing sector suffers because their goods become less competitive than like-for-like imports. For the past five years the GCC has been experiencing an economic boom – the most sustained throughout this book's period of study, primarily on the back of the phenomenal increase in both oil prices and demand since 2002 (see Figure 2.1).

One consequence of 'Dutch disease' is that until recently at least, the role of the non-oil private sector has been limited. This in turn exacerbates the region's procyclical ('boom–bust') economic performance: when oil prices slide, there are few non-oil dependent sectors to soften the fall. The region's procyclical economic performance is evidenced by an analysis of GCC GDP growth rates. They show high levels of volatility, high standard deviations and large coefficients of variation from the long-run average. Such economic uncertainty makes fiscal planning and longer term investment decisions more difficult to make. The more diversified economies of the MENA region have standard deviations and coefficient of variations of less than half that of the GCC.

The bloc's oil endowment has also resulted in it exhibiting many of the 'rentier state' characteristics as defined by Beblawi and Luciani (1987). While there is nothing wrong with distributing oil wealth among citizens, some delivery methods can have unintended consequences and at times be counterproductive.

Table 2.2 Selected GCC oil and gas indicators, 2006

	Bahrain	*Kuwait*	*Oman*	*Qatar*	*KSA*	*UAE*	*GCC*
Share of global proven oil reserves	<0.05%	8.4%	0.5%	1.3%	21.9%	8.1%	40.2%
Oil reserves per capita ('000 bbls)	0.17	34.21	2.25	18.13	11.15	19.41	13.55
Expected life of oil reserves (years)	7.13	102.77	20.53	36.76	66.63	90.19	72.06
Share of global natural gas reserves	<0.05%	1.0%	0.5%	14.0%	3.9%	3.3%	22.7%
Gas reserves per capita (mcm)	0.12	0.60	0.40	30.23	0.30	1.20	1.16
Expected life of gas reserves (years)	8.14	137.98	39.00	512.34	95.97	127.90	188.21
Oil and gas as a share of GDP[a]	25.3%	54.5%	49.2%	59.6%	48.1%	35.5%	45.3%
Oil and gas as share of government revenues	75.7%[a]	94.8%	79.1%[a]	67.1%[a]	89.5%	69.4%[a]	79.3%
Oil and gas as share of total exports	79.7%	94.5%[a]	84.2%[a]	87%	89.6%[a]	69.1%[ab]	84.1%

Source: Author's calculations based on data from AMF (2006); BP (2007); Energy Information Administration (2007); National Bank of Kuwait (2007); IMF (2007a).

Notes

a Data for 2005.

b Excludes re-exports.

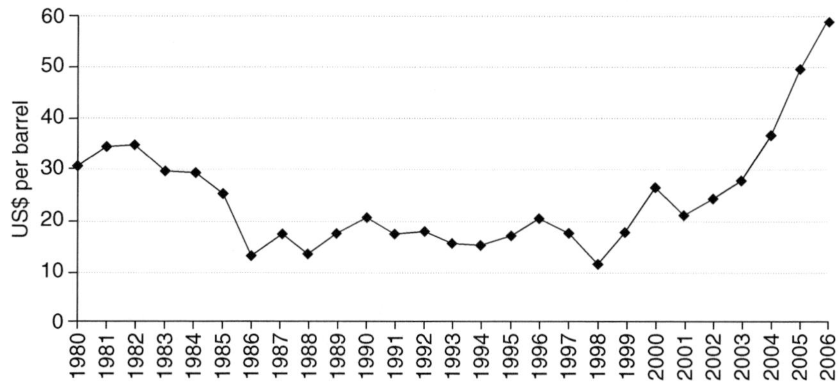

Figure 2.1 Average price of Persian Gulf crude oil, 1980–2006 (source: IEA (2007).

Note
The Persian Gulf basket of crudes includes oil from the following states, Bahrain, Iran, Iraq, Kuwait, Qatar, Saudi Arabia and the United Arab Emirates.

Two examples come to mind, one recent and (probably) short lived, the other long running and partially responsible for what we consider to be one of the bloc's biggest economic challenges.

The first was the partial listings of government owned entities on the region's bourses, most notably in 2005. In many instances only nationals were eligible to buy shares at the IPO stage; they were considerably underpriced and as soon as they were openly traded multiplied in value. Arguably the intention was not just distribute some of the recent oil windfall revenues to citizens, but also to encourage them to see the Gulf's stock market as a viable alternative to depositing their savings in overseas bank accounts. Yet these huge overnight gains led to a bull market coupled with blind speculation across the board (see Chapter 3), and when inevitably, the correction came in early 2006, it was predominantly local retail investors who ended up losing out.

The second has been providing nationals with well-remunerated public sector employment for the most part, irrespective of merit. This has led to considerable labour market distortions: a well-paid but unproductive public sector staffed by nationals and a lower paid, but competitive private sector staffed by expatriates. It is also resulting in an ever larger wage bill (recurrent fiscal burden). It has been reported that some Gulf nationals prefer to remain *unemployed* and hold out for a public sector position rather than consider the many private sector openings. This is not so surprising if one considers the UAE government's decision in November 2007 to give *all* federal government employees a 70 per cent pay increase, this is on top of a 2005 pay increase for the same sector which gave nationals a 25 per cent increase and expatriates a 15 per cent increase, irrespective of time served or productivity levels. Likewise in 2005, Saudi Arabia gave *all* government employees a 15 per cent pay rise.

It must be said that not all 'resource-rich, labour-poor' states with large resource endowments share similar traits or have such procyclical economies; Norway is an example. Like the GCC it has a relatively small population – very high per capita oil reserves – earns considerable external rent and has a modern infrastructure and a generous welfare system. Unlike the GCC however, Norway has a more robust non-oil economy and furthermore levies considerable taxes on its citizens. It should be said in fairness that Norway's economy was already reasonably developed and diversified prior to its discovery of oil.

Economic performance

The emerging BRIC economies are widely considered to have the best growth potentials in the coming decades; can the GCC be considered in a similar vein? Admittedly it has a far smaller population – and hence domestic market – but like Russia and Brazil (after Petrobras' recent oil discoveries off of the Rio de Janeiro coastline), its huge resource endowment may be able to guarantee it above emerging market average growth rates for the next few decades. In 2006 the GCC economies were among the fastest growing in the world – collectively they had double digit nominal economic growth of 24 per cent and huge current account surpluses on aggregate amounting to $176 billion (see Table 2.1). Yet, for much of the period of analysis it was a different story, during the 1980s and 1990s GCC economic performance was characterized by lacklustre growth and at times falling per capita incomes.

The 1980s

Following the oil price spikes of the 1970s these states along with many other OPEC members invested some of the windfall earnings back into their respective hydrocarbons sectors and therefore increased net global production. This soon led to a glut of oil on the world market and resulted in prices falling precipitously. It took the next two decades for the demand-supply balance to move back in favour of the suppliers. Between 1980 and 1986 the price of regional crudes fell by 57 per cent (see Figure 2.1). As a consequence many of these economies witnessed periods of recession, suffering consecutive years of double digit negative growth and large financial imbalances. In 1982, the bloc's aggregate GDP contracted by 11 per cent. In short, the 'booms' of the 1970s were followed by the 'busts' of the 1980s.

By 1986, all six states were suffering from large fiscal deficits, which, with the exception of Bahrain and the UAE, constituted more than 20 per cent of their respective GDPs. In response most initiated large cutbacks in capital outlays. It was at this time that the need for economic diversification was seen by policymakers as an imperative. In the second half of the 1980s the oil price recovered somewhat and growth rates eventually returned to positive territory. Nevertheless, policies and economic plans were increasingly geared towards achieving more balanced and sustainable growth. Despite such policies, for the decade as a whole the average aggregate growth rate of GDP was negative at –1.3 per cent

Table 2.3 GCC GDP growth averages and volatility (per cent), 1980–2006

	1980–1989	*1990–1999*	*2000–2006*	*Standard deviation*	*Coefficient of variation*
Bahrain	3.9	4.9	6.0	3.0	0.6
Kuwait	–1.6	2.5	7.9	17.1	7.1
Oman	7.5	4.9	4.9	5.7	1.0
Qatar	0.3	5.2	8.4	9.7	2.3
Saudi Arabia	–1.7	3.1	4.2	5.6	3.5
UAE	0.0	5.4	8.1	7.6	1.8
GCC	–1.3	3.2	5.8	4.6	2.1
MENA	2.3	2.2	3.9	2.3	0.7

Source: Author's calculations based on data from IMF (2007a); MENA data from World Bank (2007a).

Notes
Annual percentage growth rate of GDP based on constant prices. Standard deviation and coefficient of variation calculated for entire period.
Standard deviation is a measure of the distribution of the data around its mean. Coefficient of variation is another measure of distribution, defined as the ratio of the standard deviation to the mean.

(see Table 2.3) and living standards, measured by their per capita GDPs, actually declined by 0.7 per cent annually.

The 1990s

The 1991 Gulf war heralded a political and security crisis at the beginning of the decade which not only (and obviously) had adverse economic repercussions for Kuwait, but also for Saudi Arabia – as the latter felt compelled to bankroll most of the hugely expensive American-led campaign. In Kuwait's 1990–1991 financial year, its budget deficit was estimated to have exceeded 100 per cent of GDP and in 1991 Saudi Arabia's deficit rose to 17 per cent of GDP. Following a brief war-induced spike, oil prices soon retreated to the doldrums. Nevertheless economic performance recovered somewhat compared to the previous decade and GDP grew at an average annual rate of 3.2 per cent during the 1990s (see Table 2.3). Yet, these increases only just kept pace with population growth, which itself averaged three per cent over the decade. In 1998 the price of oil fell to its lowest point during the period of analysis, consequently the GCC recording its lowest year on year GDP growth rate for the decade in 1999 at just 0.3 per cent.

As a consequence if this lacklustre growth all states committed themselves to structural reform programmes and instituted economic diversification plans. Many sought to reduce the role of the public sector and also talked of privatizing some state-owned entities (mainly utilities and telecommunication), in order to stimulate private sector growth with the hope that this would lead to non-government-led job creation.

For example one of the aims of Saudi Arabia's sixth development plan

(1995–2000) stated was 'to rationalize government expenditure and make the national economy more dependent on private sector activities'. Increasing the private sector's economic role not only had the perceived advantage of reducing the state's fiscal burden but would also attract greater levels of FDI and facilitate the economic diversification process. Yet by 1999 Saudi Arabia's public debt amounted to 102 per cent of its GDP.

2000–2007

The far reaching economic integration plans that were set out in the 2001 Economic Agreement were in part a coordinated policy response to the region's overdependence on oil and poor performance over the previous two decades. However, as oil prices began to climb rapidly in 2002 the imperative to carry out reform was eroded somewhat, one possible objective of privatization (i.e. the need to raise cash) was no longer relevant as the GCC now began to accrue huge surpluses. Yet in spite of this fortuitous turn of events, the fundamental structural problems were still largely in place. In the 2005–2006 financial year oil and gas income constituted more than 45 per cent of GDP, almost 80 per cent of GCC government revenues and 84 per cent of total exports (see Table 2.2).

Since 2000, real economic growth has averaged 5.8 per cent, almost double that of the 1990s (see Table 2.3) and average per capita incomes (adjusted for PPP) have increased by four per cent annually. Even the non-OPEC members – Bahrain and Oman – have benefited from the general increase in liquidity and higher levels of intra-regional investment. Most notably and unlike during previous oil price booms when many of the surplus revenues were either invested or spent in the US economy ('petrodollar recycling'), significant amounts of capital have been retained and invested domestically. Some contend that this was in part due to the '9/11 factor' indeed some Arab-owned assets were frozen, it can also be attributed to the policy reforms that have taken place particularly in states such as Qatar and the UAE which have led to far more investment opportunities for domestic companies in the construction and service sectors.

Furthermore government investment in a range of infrastructure is boosting investor confidence both domestic and international. There are far fewer white elephant projects this time round and in their place are major port and airport expansions, investment parks and FTZs and even a string of 'economic cities'. In previous oil price booms GCC spending was characterized by conspicuous and unproductive consumption (Aburish 1995) including often unnecessary military purchases (Looney 2001). During the current one, on the whole, GCC states are acting more prudently, most governments are still basing fiscal budgets and spending plans on conservative oil price forecasts and Saudi Arabia is paying down its once substantial public debt, by 2006 it had been reduced by over 75 percent and now amounts to only a quarter of its GDP.

Ultimately the ability of the hydrocarbon sector to drive the economic development of these economies depends upon the spending decisions and economic policies of the region's leaders. During periods of high oil prices windfall revenues could be held back (placed into oil stabilization funds) in an attempt to protect the non-oil private sector from inflationary pressures and loss of competitiveness. Likewise during times of low oil prices – utilizing the capital accumulated in oil stabilization funds – governments could aid the private sector by continuing to offer it contracts and upgrade basic infrastructure.

The UAE has been able to avoid issuing sovereign debt as a result of such stabilization funds, it has at least four (a.k.a. sovereign wealth funds) the most noteworthy, the Abu Dhabi Investment Authority is thought to be four times the size of the world's second largest government controlled investment vehicle the China Investment Corporation (which is said to have more than $200 billion of funds to invest). In December 2007 Saudi Arabia announced plans to establish its own sovereign wealth fund that is 'expected to dwarf Abu Dhabi's $900 billion and become the largest in the world' (Sender *et al.* 2007). Until now the Saudi Arabian Monetary Authority (the Saudi central bank) had been putting much of the surplus capital it has directly into US treasury bonds. The geopolitical implications are as yet unclear, but it is safe to say that the American government can no longer count on these states to purchase all of the public debt it issues.

Structure of GDP

The structure of GCC GDP by income has changed little over the period of analysis and continues to be dominated by hydrocarbons and the public sector. Growth of the non-hydrocarbon sectors of these economies is also influenced by oil, as oil price shocks stimulate changes in public and private consumption and investment. We consider that the GCC has been diversifying over the period of study but acknowledge that the recent oil price rises distort and in a sense obscure this fact.

During the 1980s non-oil growth in all of the GCC states outstripped that of the wider economy (see Figure 2.2). More recently rising oil prices and production have been the principal growth drivers in the wider economy and are once again overtaking growth in the non-oil sectors. The possible exception to this is the UAE where its diversification process has been by far the region's most dynamic and successful. It is apparent from the following analysis of GDP structure that economic diversification has also been pursued diligently in Bahrain and Oman, which, unlike the UAE, have limited oil reserves and hence little choice but to concentrate on these sectors for future growth prospects.

An analysis of GCC national accounts shows that oil and gas extraction, often categorized as 'mining, quarrying and fuel', has been the largest contributing sector to GDP since 1980 and continues to constitute the single most important economic sector in these economies. 'Government services' also consistently ranks high, indicating the dominance of the public sector. Nevertheless, there has been some evidence of diversification occurring most notably in the manufacturing and service sectors. The manufacturing sector has increased as a proportion of GDP in all GCC states since 1980 and by 2005 it was the third largest contributor (see Tables 2.4 and 2.5).

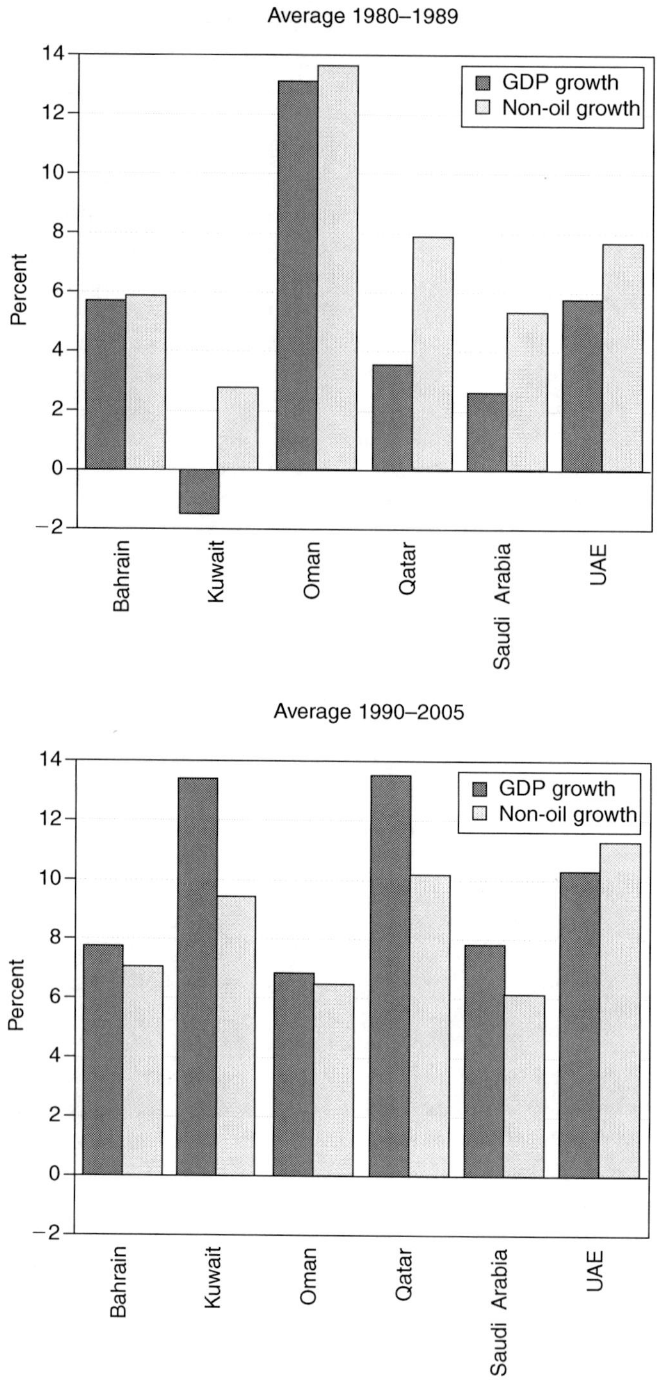

Figure 2.2 GCC nominal GDP and non-oil growth, 1980–2005 (source: Author's calculations based on data from AMF (2006 and various years)).

Table 2.4 GCC GDP distribution by sector (per cent), 1980

	Bahrain	*Kuwait*	*Oman*	*Qatar*	*KSA*	*UAE*
Agriculture, fishing and forestry	1.0	0.2	2.5	0.5	1.1	0.8
Mining, quarrying and fuel	30.5	65.6	62.1	67.2	66.1	64.4
Manufacturing industries	14.7	5.5	0.8	3.3	4.0	3.8
Electricity, water and gas	0.8	–1.0	0.8	0.2	0.1	1.2
Construction	6.9	3.6	5.7	5.4	9.8	9.0
Goods – producing industries	53.9	73.9	71.9	76.6	81.1	79.2
Commerce, hotels and restaurants	11.4	7.7	9.1	4.5	4.3	8.3
Transport comm. and storage	7.9	2.3	1.9	1.4	3.5	3.4
Banking, finance and insurance	9.9	6.7	0.5	6.0	1.2	4.3
Government services	9.7	–	9.4	–	5.8	5.5
Housing	4.7	–	5.2	–	2.4	–
Other services	2.4	8.5	1.7	11.4	1.1	0.9
Service industries	46.0	25.2	27.8	23.3	18.3	22.4
Net indirect taxes	0.0	0.8	0.4	–	0.5	–1.5
GDP at purchaser's values	100	100	100	100	100	100

Source: Author's calculations based on historical data from AMF(1980).

Table 2.5 GCC GDP distribution by sector (per cent), 2005

	Bahrain	*Kuwait*	*Oman*	*Qatar*	*KSA*	*UAE*
Agriculture, fishing and forestry	0.4	0.3	1.5	0.1	3.3	2.2
Mining, quarrying and fuel	25.3	54.5	49.2	59.6	48.1	35.5
Manufacturing industries	12.7	7.4	8.5	8.4	9.6	12.5
Electricity, water and gas	1.3	1.3	1.3	1.4	0.9	1.6
Construction	3.4	1.9	2.5	5.7	4.7	7.1
Goods – producing industries	43.1	65.4	63.0	75.2	66.6	58.9
Commerce, hotels and restaurants	10.4	4.9	11.0	4.4	5.4	12.6
Transport comm., and storage	6.0	5.5	5.9	3.3	3.3	6.7
Banking, finance and insurance	24.4	4.4	1.0	9.6	4.1	4.3
Government services	2.5	12.8	7.4	8.0	14.4	7.1
Housing	5.8	3.5	2.9	–	4.3	7.3
Other services	3.6	2.7	8.1	–1.7	1.0	2.0
Service industries	52.7	33.8	36.3	23.6	32.5	40.0
Net indirect taxes	4.2	0.8	0.7	1.2	0.9	1.1
GDP at purchaser's values	100	100	100	100	100	100

Source: Author's calculations based on data from AMF (2006).

Manufacturing sector

The manufacturing sector's contribution to GDP in 2005 was the greatest in Bahrain followed by the UAE. As all of the GCC states have a competitive advantage in energy-heavy industrial processes, such as aluminium and steel production and petrochemicals, investment into them has grown substantially since 2002. For instance, Dubal (a UAE government-controlled aluminium producer), in conjunction with Mubadala (another UAE sovereign investment fund), is investing $6 billion in expanding its aluminium production capacity at an existing smelter – which, when complete it will be one of the world's largest. Qatar and Oman are also both working with foreign partners to construct new aluminium smelters.

The GCC's upstream refining sector is also currently receiving huge public and private investments. Both Kuwait and the UAE are planning ambitious developments that are expected to increase their capacity in this sector by 60 and 40 per cent respectively (Luciani 2007). GCC-wide investment in downstream petrochemical production capacity is projected to double between 2006 and 2015 and Saudi Arabia is set to become one of the largest petrochemical producers in the world. These developments are likely to increase opportunities for a wide range of smaller scale manufacturing companies across the region. As we consider many of these as 'value-added' industries, by the governments investing in these sectors, they should better insulate themselves against any future downturn in the price of oil.

Service sector

Both Bahrain and the UAE have also been relatively successful in building their service sectors. Taken as a whole their service sectors now comprise a larger proportion of their national economies at 53 and 40 per cent of GDP respectively in 2005 than their oil and gas sectors. Within the service sector, 'banking, finance and insurance' constitutes the major share in Bahrain and in 2005 the financial services sector was the second largest contributor to Bahraini GDP at 24 per cent (it formed just ten per cent of GDP in 1980). In Qatar over the same period financial services grew from six per cent to ten per cent.

In recent years Bahrain, Qatar and the Emirate of Dubai have all invested heavily in their financial service sectors, establishing new 'global financial hubs' and liberalizing their respective banking and finance regulations in order to attract foreign banks – with, it should be said, some considerable success. The Qatar Financial Centre and the Dubai International Finance Centre are both government backed and are buying large stakes in some of the world's key bourses.

For instance, the Qatar Investment Authority, Qatar's sovereign wealth fund, purchased a 20 per cent stake in the London Stock Exchange and Dubai Bourse has acquired a stake in NASDAQ. Such investments will not only raise the profile of these emerging stock markets but should also facilitate a knowledge and technical transfer. With more of the region's family-owned companies choosing to list and the meteoric rise of the Islamic debt (*sukuk*) market, the financial services sector offers these states with considerable diversification opportunities.

With globally recognized airlines such as Emirates and Qatar Airways, the region is increasingly trying to position itself not just a transport hub 'bridging Asia and Europe', but also as a tourist and business conference destination in its own right. The tourism sector (defined in most national accounts as 'commerce, hotels and restaurants') already contributes significantly to the economies of Oman and the UAE and is a potentially sustainable non-oil dependent source of income. This sector accounted for 11 per cent and 12.6 per cent of GDP in 2005 in Oman and the UAE respectively, growing from 9.1 per cent and 8.3 per cent of their GDP in 1980.

Many of the headline-grabbing projects in Dubai such as the three palms and a constellation of islands that map out the world (if viewed from outer space) all built on reclaimed land are part and parcel of the UAE's plan of becoming a major tourist destination. British holidaymakers already seem enamoured, evidenced by more than a dozen daily direct flights between the two countries. Potentials for intra-GCC tourism are even greater. Traditionally, most Gulf Arabs spent their summer holidays in Beirut, Geneva or London; far more Saudis are now choosing to simply drive over to Dubai. Intra-GCC investment in this sector is substantial, many of the projects taking shape in Bahrain and Oman are being funded by Saudi and Emirati businesses.

Monetary policy and inflation

For much of the period of analysis inflation rates have been well contained, on average under 3 per cent, yet this masks periods of considerable volatility and divergence between countries. These generally low inflation rates are attributable to three main factors: monetary policy credibility, extensive price subsidies and a large expatriate labour force. Some of the regional experts we interviewed argued that following the monetary decisions of the US Federal Reserve provides the GCC's central banks with 'more credibility'. It was further argued that since GCC central banks are relatively inexperienced a managed float would be difficult to deal with and, therefore, delegating monetary policy to the Federal Reserve at this stage of their economic development is prudent.

Monetary policy

In one shape or form the GCC states have pegged their respective currencies to the dollar for several decades and consequently their interest rates have followed those of the US, Kuwait being the notable exception. Throughout most of the period of analysis the Kuwaiti dinar has been pegged to a basket of currencies (no doubt having a significant dollar component, some estimate it to be at least 70 per cent). The Omani rial has been officially pegged to the dollar since the 1970s; the Bahraini dinar, Qatari rial, Saudi riyal and the Emirati dirham were all pegged to the IMF's Special Drawing Rights (a basket of currencies with a heavy dollar weighting).[1] In 2003 Kuwait joined the other GCC states in adopting a *de jure* dollar peg, in order to synchronize exchange rates prior to MU. The Kuwaiti dinar was the only currency allowed a band of adjustment at ±3.5 per cent until the scheduled monetary unification which it utilized to the full in the following years. Yet in May 2007 Kuwait moved back to its former trade-weighted basket peg citing the need to fight 'imported inflation'.

Exchange rate fixing has important implications for the ability of the domestic authorities to control their inflation environment. On the one hand, it is argued that the fixed pegs have prevented a nominal appreciation of the GCC currencies, which may have exacerbated inflationary pressures in these economies. On the other, however, it is contended that pegging to a major trading currency can reduce the inflation-bias problem often experienced in transitional economies (Barro and Gordon 1983; Ghosh *et al.* 1997). Yet the US real effective exchange rate[2] has been relatively volatile which may at times have harmed the competitiveness and growth of non-oil GCC exports (Esquivel and Larrain 2002). Therefore the bloc's exchange rates choices have not necessarily provided them with the degree of exchange rate stability which is often assumed (see Chapter 8 for more discussion of this).

Fixing exchange rates to an external anchor has meant that interest rate setting as a monetary policy tool has not been available for use (see Table 2.6 for a summary of the limited monetary tools currently in use). In our view a key problem with this arrangement is interest rates for the US domestic economy are often not appropriate for the GCC. In the second half of 2007, US interest rates were being cut, in response to the credit crunch and falling American house prices. The GCC central banks had to follow suit yet with oil prices hovering around the $90/b mark a rate hike would have been more appropriate.

Inflation rates

Although as we have pointed out over the long-run levels of aggregate inflation have been low (see Table 2.7) there have been significant peaks in particular states and in fact the GCC have faced considerable volatility in their inflation rates. Short-run peaks in inflation in the GCC economies have coincided with two phenomena: high oil prices and/or a depreciation of the dollar. Strong oil prices at the beginning of the 1980s pushed GCC inflation to a decade high of 7.4 per cent in 1981. Between 1985 and the end of 1990 the dollar's trade-weighted value fell by 36 per cent at the same time GCC average inflation rates rose gradually from –0.5 per cent in 1985 to 2.25 per cent in 1989. In the following year, an oil price spike caused by the Persian Gulf war saw average inflation rise to 5.5 per cent in 1991. But due to stagnant oil prices throughout much of the 1990s average inflation rates for the decade were low at only 2.2 per cent (see Table 2.7). Since 2002 as rising oil prices have coincided with a period of US dollar weakness, inflation rates throughout the GCC have been on an upward trajectory and in Qatar and the UAE, where real interest rates had turned negative, inflation had reached double-digit figures (see Table 2.1).

Since 2001 oil prices have almost trebled while the dollar has fallen by about 20 per cent against a broad index of currencies and approximately 60 per cent against the euro (Blas and Kerr 2007). A depreciation of the dollar, and concomitantly GCC currencies, causes the price of imports from non-dollar trading blocs to increase. The GCC states have high import propensities and low price elasticities of demand for imports (Mohammad and El-Sakka 2001), con-

Table 2.6 GCC monetary policy tools

	Reserve requirements	*Open market operations*	*Central bank paper*	*Primary market sales of government securities*
Bahrain	Unremunerated; 5 per cent on dinar deposits	Repos with treasury bills; foreign exchange swaps	No	Yes, treasury bills and development bonds
Kuwait	Unremunerated; reserve ratio based on maturity	Liquidity scheme; foreign exchange swaps, deposit operations	No	Yes, treasury bills and government bonds
Oman	Unremunerated; 5 per cent on domestic and foreign currency deposits	Repos, foreign exchange swaps	Yes	Yes, treasury bills and development bonds
Qatar	Unremunerated; cash reserves of 2.75 per cent of total deposits	Repos and deposit facility (Qatar monetary rate mechanism)	No	Yes, treasury bills and government bonds
KSA	Unremunerated; 9 per cent[a] on demand deposits and 2 per cent on time deposits	Repos, foreign exchange swaps	No	Yes, treasury bills and government bonds
UAE	Unremunerated; 1 per cent on time deposits and 14 per cent on current deposits	Foreign exchange swaps, repos/reserve repos being developed	Yes	Yes, some federal governments bonds have been issued post 2002[b]

Source: Adapted from Fasano and Staff Team (2003).

Notes

a This was increased to 9 per cent in November 2007, it had been set at 7 per cent for the previous 27 years.

b In 2003 the government of Dubai set a precedent by launching the UAE's first government bond issue worth US$400mn.

Table 2.7 GCC inflation averages and volatility (per cent), 1980–2006

	1980–1989	*1990–1999*	*2000–2006*	*Standard deviation*	*Coefficient of variation*
Bahrain	2.3	0.8	1.0	3.1	2.2
Kuwait	3.6	3.1	2.0	2.9	0.9
Oman	1.0	1.6	0.5	3.5	3.2
Qatar	3.8	2.9	4.7	3.0	0.8
KSA	0.1	1.3	0.3	2.0	3.5
UAE	4.6	3.6	4.8	2.3	0.5
GCC	2.6	2.2	2.2	2.0	0.9
MENA	9.3	7.6	4.7	4.5	0.6

Source: Author's calculations based on data from IMF (2007a); MENA data from World Bank (2007a).

Note
Annual inflation rate of consumer price indices, data for Oman and the United Arab Emirates begins from 1981. MENA inflation rate calculated from GDP deflator and ends 2005.

sequently rising import prices have a significant impact on the general domestic price level and inflation in these countries.

Using econometric analysis Ghars El-Din and Mohammad (2005) found that a ten per cent depreciation causes a 2.1–7.4 per cent rise in GCC domestic prices. The combination of low price elasticities of demand for imports and the absence of a well-established import substitution sector implies that domestic prices in the GCC states are more sensitive to a changes in import prices resulting from a devaluation of their currencies than they are to domestic economic conditions. Substantial increases in regional liquidity have also taken place. In 2005 for example, broad money supply increases were in double-digit figures in each of the GCC states and reached a high of 38 per cent in Qatar followed by 34 per cent in the UAE, resulting in a region-wide asset price boom.

Of direct relevance to the subject of this and monetary convergence in particular since the beginning of this decade GCC inflation rates have once again been diverging (see Chapter 4). There are considerable differences between GCC inflation rates, for example since 2000 average inflation in the UAE and Qatar has been 4.8 and 4.7 per cent respectively, whereas Saudi Arabia and Oman recorded almost negligible inflation rates at just 0.3 per cent and 0.5 per cent respectively (see Table 2.7).

Trade and investment

The GCC states are generally considered to be open trading economies; all are now WTO members. One could characterize the overall pattern of GCC trade as the exportation of oil and gas – constituting on average more than four-fifths of total exports – and the importation of manufactured goods – representing 77 per cent of total imports (UN 2006). As many items are relatively cheaper to import from outside of the bloc, intra-GCC trade has, up until now, been rather limited. In 2006 intra-GCC imports constituted only 7.9 per cent of total GCC imports, yet the value of imports has grown annually by 6.8 per cent over the period of analysis.

In 1994 oil and gas made up just over three-quarters of total exports; by 2006 this had actually increased to 84 per cent. Taken at face value this indicates that the GCC has become less diversified, not more; however, the extreme volatility of the oil price can seriously distort the picture. For example, in 1998 oil and gas exports as a proportion of total exports fell to 67 per cent suggesting that the GCC was substantially diversifying its exports but this occurred at a time when oil prices were at their lowest point in the period of study.

In 2005 Saudi Arabia's exports of chemical products represented 6.1 per cent of its total exports (including oil), its largest export following petroleum products, whereas in 1985 the proportion had been just 2 per cent (ESCWA 2001). In Qatar, exports of chemical products formed 5.2 per cent of their total exports in 2005, second only to petroleum and natural gas exports. In the same year Bahrain's aluminium exports accounted for 10.8 per cent of its total exports.

Bahrain stands out from the other GCC states witnessing several negative trade balances over the last two decades. Between 1980 and 2006, Bahrain experienced 11 years of trade deficits and a period of successive trade deficits from 1983 to 1989 as well as from 1991 to 1994. Due to its limited oil and gas reserves, Bahrain is now reliant on imports of crude oil from Saudi Arabia in order to fuel its energy-intensive manufacturing sector, including the aluminium smelting industry. Since 1998 the UAE has been the only GCC state to experience several years of trade deficits; between 2004 and 2006 it continuously ran a trade deficit as imports surged by an annual rate of 43 per cent, compared to export growth of 31 per cent.

The value of GCC export earnings has been growing on average by 30 per cent annually since 2002 and had reached approximately $424 billion in 2006 (IMF 2007b). In addition to the increase in export earnings, the value of imports to the GCC states has also witnessed significant growth in recent years, increasing annually by 24 per cent on aggregate over the same period to reach $238 billion in 2006. Overall, the average trade surpluses of the GCC states as a percentage of their GDP between 1980 and 2006 ranged from a minimum of 14.3 per cent in the case of Bahrain to a maximum of 31.8 per cent in Qatar.

Looking East, trade with Asia grows

Asia is now the GCC's most important export partner, with 37.5 per cent of total GCC exports destined to Asia in 2006, compared to just 10 and 9 per cent to the EU and US respectively. The *share* of GCC exports to the US has declined slightly since 1980, while the *value* of exports has only grown by an annual rate of 2.7 per cent. The *share* of GCC exports to the EU has fallen considerably over the same period as has the actual *value*, which has decreased by an annual rate of 1.2 per cent since 1980. In comparison the *share and value* of GCC

Table 2.8 GCC direction of trade, 1980–2006

	Share (%) of GCC imports by origin				
	1980	*1990*	*2000*	*2006*	*Ann. growth over period*
Asia	11.2	15.0	21.2	27.9	9.8
European Union	37.2	34.0	32.1	29.4	5.1
US	16.7	13.0	13.1	11.4	4.5
Intra-GCC	6.6	8.4	8.7	7.9	6.8
Rest of world	28.3	29.7	25.0	23.5	6.0
	Share (%) of GCC exports by destination				
	1980	*1990*	*2000*	*2006*	*Ann. growth over period*
Asia	14.8	19.6	33.9	37.5	7.7
European Union	36.7	14.8	11.4	9.9	–1.2
US	11.7	14.4	10.7	8.7	2.7
Intra-GCC	3.0	8.0	4.9	4.7	5.8
Rest of world	33.8	43.2	39.2	39.2	3.9

Source: Author's calculations based on data from IMF (2007b).

exports to Asia have increased substantially by 7.7 per cent over the last 25 years (see Table 2.8).

On average between 1999 and 2005, the largest share of oil exports from the four GCC OPEC members were destined to Asia and the Pacific, in the case of the UAE and Qatar the share was as high as 97 and 80 per cent; for Kuwait and Saudi Arabia the share was slightly lower yet still significant at 72 and 49 per cent.[3] Asian states have recognized the importance of their trading relationship with the GCC and most are in the process of negotiating FTAs with the bloc. Both China and India signed framework agreements on economic, trade, investment and technological cooperation with the GCC, in 2004.

On the import side of the GCC trade balance, in 2006 the largest share of GCC imports originated from Europe and Asia, accounting for 29 and 28 per cent of total imports respectively. While the value of imports from the US and the EU grew moderately at an annual rate of 4.5 and 5.1 per cent respectively between 1980 and 2006 in contrast those from Asia increased annually by 9.8 per cent in the same period. The GCC is the EU's sixth largest export market and a wide range of European manufactured goods are consumed in the GCC. However, it appears that the continuing decline in GCC purchasing power of euro-denominated imports has led to some import diversification as the share of imports from the EU has fallen recently (in 2004 it was 3 per cent higher at 32 per cent of total GCC imports).

Investment trends

Traditionally, FDI into the GCC has been limited by factors such as the small size of the domestic markets, the extensive public sector control over large swathes of the economy and legal restrictions limiting foreign ownership of companies. This is particularly the case with regard to the upstream oil and gas industries, in part due to political considerations but also the inherent need to control the rate of resource depletion and adhere to OPEC quotas. On average between 2001 and 2005 the GCC states received just 1.2 per cent of global FDI (UN 2006) over the period, their dollar peg exchange rate mechanism has not discernibly assisted them in attracting FDI inflows. Recently, however, things have started to change, inward investment has grown considerably, rising from just $2.3 billion in 2001 to more than $20 billion in 2005.

FDI in the downstream hydrocarbon sector is now being actively encouraged, often in order to gain exposure to sophisticated technology. Since 2004 Saudi Arabia has signed a string of deals with foreign oil and petrochemical companies. The largest single to date was Saudi Aramco's (the state-owned oil giant) agreement with Japan's Sumitomo Chemical to build what is to be the world's largest integrated refinery and petrochemicals complex – PetroRabigh (Rutledge 2006b). In May 2006, for example, two major deals with international oil companies – ConocoPhillips of the US and France's Total – were signed. Both agreements were for jointly constructing multibillion dollar refineries, together totalling $12 billion (Ghafour 2006). Also, Oman's current Five-year Plan (2001–2006) makes clear that private and often foreign investment in a number of gas-based projects is essential if its objectives are to be met. The plan hopes to attract a total of $11.4 billion in private sector investment compared to the estimated $4.9 billion it received between 1996 and 2000 (UNDP 2007).

Economic mass is often considered to be an important determinant for FDI; it is not therefore surprising to find that on average the two largest GCC economies, Saudi Arabia and the UAE, attracted the greatest shares of FDI between 2001 and 2005, at 18 and 58 per cent respectively. Yet Qatar, one of the smallest GCC states, also attracted a significant proportion of FDI, accounting for 12 per cent of total GCC FDI inflows over the same period. A more meaningful measure of FDI is as a share of GDP, in this case the GCC's two most diversified economies – the UAE and Bahrain, attracted the most significant levels of FDI in 2005, amounting to 9.3 and 7.8 per cent of their GDP respectively. Qatar was in third place with its FDI equating to 4.3 per cent of its GDP.

The UAE in particular, has been proactive in implementing policies to attract foreign investors, enacting laws to allow foreign investment in real estate and running successful marketing campaigns advertising as an ideal location for business. In particular Dubai has been active in establishing several FTZs, which also provide incentives for foreign companies to establish themselves, such as allowing 100 per cent foreign ownership and profit repatriation; this policy has attracted many multinational companies to Dubai and has spurred FDI. The UAE, along with Bahrain, has also seen relative success in its diversification into the service sector. Generally considered to be the most liberal of the GCC states, the UAE has been able to attract foreign companies and workers easily and allowing foreigners to purchase property in designated areas has also improved the business climate for FDI. Again acting as a regional trendsetter many states are now, like the UAE, permitting foreigners to purchase villas and apartments in designated zones (often on reclaimed land). This trend is not, however, being followed in Saudi Arabia.

Despite being the largest economy of the group by far, FDI as a percentage of Saudi Arabia's GDP amounted to just 1.5 per cent in 2005, only higher than that for Kuwait which was 0.3 per cent of GDP. Nevertheless, since 2004 Saudi Arabia has made serious efforts to attract increased investment by cutting the corporation taxes it levies on some foreign companies from 45 per cent to 20 per cent (*Arab News* 2004b). Following its accession to the WTO Saudi Arabia announced that is would give licences to ten foreign banks to operate in its domestic market.

Key economic challenges

While the GCC's resource wealth has afforded rapid economic development within a short period of time it is not without cost, some consider oil windfalls to be a 'mixed blessing' (Ross 1999). Such windfalls have led to an overreliance on oil and have at times generated significant macroeconomic instability and fiscal imbalances. In another regard, as the hydrocarbon sector is firmly in the hands of the state, the public sector has taken the leading role in most economic activities, historically limiting the role of the private sector and leading to significant labour market distortions, as regional governments tended to distribute oil wealth through the provision of (over-remunerated) public sector jobs.

As a result of income dependence on oil the region often witnessed periods of consecutive fiscal deficits which during the 1980s and 1990s often amounted to more than 20 per cent of GDP (see Table 2.9). Yet, many of the challenges first identified in the 1980s, continue to preoccupy policymakers today. In 2005 for instance, Qatar announced that its main economic policy objective was to diversify the economy and increase the role of the private sector. The issue of national unemployment is much more of a problem today than it was in the 1980s as national populations have grown significantly since then, but we also believe that since 2002, the majority of the bloc's governments have made good policy decisions with respect to opening up financial, service and tourism sectors.

Scaling back the public sector

Implicit in the hydrocarbon dependence of these economies is the leading role played by the public sector which has limited the growth of the region's private sectors. In turn this resulted in large public sector spending commitments, often unsustainable during periods of low oil prices. During the 1990s budgetary

Table 2.9 GCC budget balance as a per cent of GDP, 1980–2006

	1980–1989		*1990–1999*		*2000–2006*	
	Average	*Max.*	*Average*	*Max.*	*Average*	*Max.*
Bahrain	1.4	–5.4	–3.0	–6.5	2.8	–0.1
Kuwait	–4.3	–21.7	–9.0	–27.0	19.8	+5.7
Oman	–8.7	–22.3	–7.6	–12.1	5.3	–4.8
Qatar	–2.8	–30.5	–6.5	–10.7	7.2	+2.0
KSA	–7.4	–25.3	–7.1	–10.5	6.6	–3.9
UAE	–4.3	–14.7	–9.8	–16.5	5.4	–11.3

Source: Author's calculations based on data from Al-Uwaisheg (2003); GCC central bank reports (various issues).

Note
Due to the 1991 Gulf war data for Kuwait is missing in 1990 and 1991, likewise for Saudi Arabia in 1991.

requirements were encouraging GCC states to consider partially privatize some state entities (far more were planned than actually came to fruition). Average budget deficits during the 1990s ranged from –3 per cent in Bahrain to –9.8 per cent in the UAE (see Table 2.9).

Yet since the beginning of this decade there has been no financial imperative to carry out such privatizations with most GCC states experiencing large fiscal surpluses and as many of these entities (being associated with oil) are extremely profitable; not only are they providing the treasury with substantial revenues, no other investment is likely to provide higher returns. In recent years some partial privatizations have taken place, yet as mentioned at the outset of this chapter, these are more likely to have been motivated by a desire to allow Gulf nationals to share in the enormous oil wealth currently accruing to these regimes, than to raise cash, radically overhaul their structures or streamline them by making them accountable to shareholders.

Consequently, despite various policies aimed at reducing the role of the government vis-à-vis the private sector, in most GCC states this has only taken place to a limited degree. In some GCC states, concerns over increasing national unemployment are likely to hinder the transfer of state-owned companies to the private sector as many unproductive (and at times 'ghost positions') would be shed. For example, in Kuwait the policy of privatization has faced social and political obstacles and continuous objections from members of the state's national assembly who fear that selling off state assets could eventually erode Kuwait's generous welfare state.

The situation in Kuwait illustrates an important point that in some respects there have always been built-in limitations on the extent to which a narrow form of privatization (selling off state-owned assets) could be carried out. Firstly, since the majority of state-owned assets fall within the hydrocarbon sector which is a strategic asset of vast importance to governments, there is naturally a reluctance to reduce state control over this sector. Secondly, state ownership of the oil and gas sector as well as basic utilities enables the governments to utilize these as a means of providing a range of subsidies and welfare benefits to the population – a major political economy consideration which could be prejudiced if the state lost control of the sector.

Empirical evidence on the growth of the GCC private sector is particularly scarce. Data on the breakdown of total investment into public or private sectors is not available on a comparable basis throughout the region. Nevertheless, according to the expenditure measure of GDP, public consumption in the GCC has fluctuated considerably with a small downward trend since 1980. In 1980 public consumption averaged 39 per cent overall, ranging between a low of 23 per cent in Bahrain and a high of 56 per cent in Qatar. In 2005 the average was slightly lower at 33 per cent, ranging from only 19 per cent in the UAE to 47 per cent in Saudi Arabia. Certain GCC states have been more successful at stimulating private sector consumption than others. Again Bahrain and the UAE appear to have achieved most in this regard, where the private consumption to GDP ratio was at its highest at 45 per cent of GDP in both states in 2005, where diversification efforts seem to have paid off. Over the period of analysis the UAE was the only GCC state where private consumption has at one time (in 2004) formed the majority of expenditure on GDP.

In addition to the policy of selling off state assets to the private sector, a number of other policies aimed at increasing private sector activities have been adopted. Several GCC states have improved the business environment for the private sector by investing in infrastructure and creating FTZs where local private sector businesses, as well as foreign companies, can locate.

Several GCC governments are now targeting the growth of small and medium sized enterprises (SMEs) in order to promote private sector growth and domestic entrepreneurialism. Small businesses in Saudi Arabia for example, are the main source of private sector investment and they form more than 90 per cent of private enterprises across the country (*Arab News* 2006). Consequently the Saudi Commerce and Industry Minister, Hashim Yamani, in 2006, emphasized the importance of policies to support the growth and financing of SMEs, through mechanisms such as franchising. Qatar's first industrial area specifically for SMEs is expected to become operational by 2008, according to Qatar's Ministry of Energy and Industry: 'The project is part of the authorities' efforts to provide suitable investment opportunities to local and foreign investors, as well as encouraging the local private sector' (Bibbo 2005).

Private sector access to capital in the GCC has in the past been limited to bank borrowing; however, since 2001 the region's stock markets have experienced substantial growth in capitalization and new listings. GCC governments have put in place improved regulatory frameworks for their capital markets which have helped retain regional investment, as well as encouraging family-owned businesses to list through measures such as legal reforms allowing nationals to retain the majority of shares and therefore controlling interests in their business.

Addressing national unemployment

In the 1980s and 1990s, GCC nationals could more or less count on being provided with governments jobs. Yet providing public sector employment for all new labour markets entrants is no longer tenable, for instance 56 per cent of Saudis are less than 20 years of age and will be joining the labour market in the coming period, 'necessitating the creation of around 100,000 new jobs annually' (Shah 2005). The recurrent costs attached to the existing public sector workforce already represents a considerable fiscal burden, especially considering that the ratio of working to pensionable age employees will soon start to shift. Yet as the oil industry is capital intensive the only credible option is to try to create conditions conducive of fostering non-oil dependent private sector employment growth.

Most GCC governments are trying to increase private sector employment of nationals by implementing labour nationalization policies involving imposing mandatory quotas on the private sector. However, the results appear to be mixed in terms of improved national employment prospects and could also have adverse implications for private sector competitiveness and labour market flexibility (see Chapter 3 for more details).

Many consider official unemployment figures to be somewhat unreliable preferring instead to use independent estimates. Unemployment levels across the bloc vary considerably; the unemployment rate is almost certainly highest in Bahrain, Oman and Saudi Arabia where, until recently, population growth has outpaced national income growth. Independent estimates put unemployment at 17.2 per cent in Oman, 15.2 per cent in Saudi Arabia (United Nations 2002) and between 12–15 per cent in Bahrain (Sassanpour *et al.* 1997). In Qatar there seems to be very little, if any, registered unemployment and for Kuwait and the UAE national unemployment has yet to become an issue of serious concern. Yet all of the GCC states have very young populations and therefore unemployment is likely to become more acute in the coming years. In Saudi Arabia, for example, population pressures are acute, 37 per cent of the Kingdom's 24 million people are under the age of 14 (World Bank 2006).

The need to diversify

While the 'feel-good factor' associated with periods of high oil prices may at times place economic diversification plans on the 'back burner', in the coming years the need to implement reforms that facilitate economic diversification will be essential both to ensure a more balanced and sustainable growth paradigm and to generate appropriate private sector jobs for nationals. The region's public sectors are already overstaffed and represent a significant recurrent cost to these regimes. And oil, after all, is a finite resource, its price inherently volatile and the associated upstream industry very capital, not labour intensive.

The region needs to attract more FDI not because they lack capital for investment (as noted they currently have substantial reserves themselves), but as FDI is conventionally assumed to bring technical and managerial expertise which should be transferable to domestic companies. Such knowledge 'spill-over' effects are, according to endogenous growth models, important in fostering economic development. Simplifying government red tape and improving the regulatory framework would help erode the barriers to increasing GCC FDI (Qasrawi 2004). Harmonizing the region's business and investment regulations and the formation of a common market, both in our view MU prerequisites which should aid and abet regional FDI inflows.

The degree of success in achieving economic diversification, as we have already established, has thus far been mixed. Nevertheless, we consider the Arabian Peninsula's long-running economic integration plans, which would culminate with a GCC MU, as a key component of these diversification strategies. The likely dividends arising from the creation of a common market and a single currency in terms of promoting intra-regional trade and private sector growth (see Chapter 6) may well explain why GCC leaders renewed their commitment to the 1981 economic agreement in 2001 and, despite a range of obstacles (see Chapter 5), are intent on forming an MU by 2010.

3 Is the GCC an optimal currency area?

This chapter will assess the GCC bloc against the traditional optimal currency area (OCA) criteria (Mundell 1961; McKinnon 1963; Kenen 1969). Despite its emergence in the 1960s the OCA theory continues to be a useful benchmark for evaluating the appropriateness of a given region for MU. The degree to which the GCC bloc constitutes an OCA will not only provide an indication of the utility of MU for the Arabian Peninsula, but may also influence the degree of political motivation towards turning this ambitious plan into reality.

It should be noted from the outset that even if the GCC states do not meet all of the OCA criteria adequately, this does not necessarily mean they will not be able to achieve a viable MU. The case of EMU is illustrative of this and also demonstrates the instrumental role political motivation plays (De Grauwe 1993). It is entirely plausible that if adequate political determination exists, a Gulf dinar will come into being regardless of whether or not all OCA criteria are met. Conversely, if political determination is lacking, an MU is unlikely to come to fruition even if the GCC is optimally suited economically speaking.

Despite efforts to 'operationalize' the OCA criteria (see Bayoumi and Eichengreen 1997) any assessment of whether a region is an OCA necessarily remains open to some degree of interpretation. We therefore employ various means in assessing the degree to which the GCC states meet these core criteria; in some cases, an empirical analysis is possible and in others only a qualitative assessment of the criterion can be undertaken. Furthermore, rather than simply undertaking a static analysis of the economic status of the GCC bloc vis-à-vis the OCA criteria we also examine the dynamic processes that are taking place which may affect their suitability for MU over time.

This chapter first discusses the economic theory of OCA and the original economic criteria established as the benchmark for forming a successful MU. The traditional OCA economic criteria are considered to be: the level and importance of intra-regional trade, intra-regional mobility of labour and capital, economic diversification and, finally, economic synchronization. It then goes on to assess the degree to which the six GCC states can be considered to meet each of these original OCA criteria. Oman is also included in the following analysis, despite its decision in December 2006 to opt out of the MU project. Just as the Eurozone has grown, from 11 to 13, it is entirely possible that Oman may decide to join at a later stage.

The development of OCA theory

The economic criteria for assessing the appropriateness of MU for a given region originated from the OCA theory which was developed in the 1960s. The theory was initially postulated by Mundell in 1961 and major additions were later developed by McKinnon (1963) and Kenen (1969). The main contention of the OCA theory is that there is a trade-off between the benefits accruing from sharing a single currency and the economic costs. Groups of countries with strong trading links will stand to benefit most from a single currency as they will gain substantially from the elimination of exchange rate risks and transaction costs. The main cost involved in joining an MU will be the loss of national exchange rate flexibility as an adjustment mechanism for absorbing economic shocks. Outside of MU when a country faces a negative external shock affecting it differently (asymmetrically) from its neighbours flexible exchange rates could help in adjusting to the shock (for example through a competitive depreciation of the national currency against its neighbour's currencies) theoretically allowing that country to maintain balance of payments equilibrium and full employment.

The OCA theory asserts that if certain economic criteria are met by the prospective member states then this will minimize the potential cost incurred when sharing monetary policy. For example, following a negative asymmetric economic shock to one member state, if labour and capital are sufficiently mobile then that economy can adjust (through labour migration within the bloc or smoothing income from capital assets in other member states) without the authorities having to resort to a bespoke monetary policy to tackle economic recession or high unemployment.

It was also contended that openness to trade will amplify the benefits from reducing transaction costs and that the efficiency gains resulting from a common currency are more obvious for smaller economies (McKinnon 1963), two characteristics which both hold for the GCC economies as an economic region. An additional criterion of economic diversification was also added later by Kenen (1969). If a group of countries are diversified and not highly dependent on specific industries or commodities then they will be less likely to experience asymmetric shocks affecting their respective industries. Furthermore, if prospective member states have synchronized (correlated) economic cycles they are also less likely to face the possibility of asymmetric economic shocks.

The 1990s and the process of EMU provided a good opportunity for MU theorists to apply the OCA theory empirically to a real world event. However, some criticism of the theory sprung from the difficulties involved in 'operationalizing' the various criteria. Nevertheless, a body of literature emerged which applied the OCA criteria in quantitative research in an attempt to test the applicability and validity of the theory. Research by Krugman (1993) seemed to indicate an internal contradiction in the OCA theory relating to the criteria of intra-regional trade and business cycle correlation. He claimed that increasing trade between countries would lead to greater national specialization of production which in turn would result in a weaker correlation between those countries incomes and business cycles and thus lead to increasingly asymmetric responses to supply shocks.

Research by Frankel and Rose (1996, 1997) however presented evidence of a positive correlation between bilateral trade intensity and business cycles. They argued that greater trade integration between two countries would in itself lead to convergence of income and business cycles. They concluded that trade could not be considered independently from the business cycle in assessing the suitability of a country for MU because, to an extent, they are jointly determined. Moreover, levels of trade are influenced by national trade policy, as is the degree of economic convergence between countries at any one time, therefore the criteria of significant intra-regional trade and synchronized business cycles might be considered to be 'endogenous' to the policy of forming an MU.

This 'endogeneity' argument proposed by Frankel and Rose (1997) somewhat diminished the importance attached to the OCA criteria by suggesting that even if countries are not economically suited to joining an MU *ex ante*, they will be *ex post* of joining. If we extrapolate this argument to other economic regions, it appears that any concerns regarding the appropriateness of a single monetary policy should diminish. Even if business cycles are not correlated prior to MU, it follows that they will become synchronized following membership. Yet for prospective members of an MU, relying on the 'endogeneity' argument alone may be considered too much of a leap of faith. There could for instance be cultural barriers to labour mobility or if all members export a similar commodity how much can intra-regional trade realistically be expected to grow?

Despite the limitations of the OCA criteria (Glavan 2004), including the contention that the OCA criteria are non-operational, the theory continues to provide a useful framework for policymakers and academics alike in estimating the appropriateness of MU for a given region (see for example Eichengreen 1997; Bayoumi and Mauro 1999; Chow and Kim 2003a, 2003b). To safeguard against the limitations of the OCA theory, and to make this study of practical relevance to the GCC, later chapters of this book also draw on the experience and lessons from EMU.

Intra-regional trade

Conventional analysis of intra-GCC trade levels and ratios shows that intra-GCC trade is weak, particularly when compared with the EMU region prior to 1999 (Jadresic 2002: 8). In 2006 intra-regional trade amounted to only 5.9 per cent of total GCC trade (IMF 2007b), much lower than that of the Eurozone countries prior to the establishment of MU where intra-regional trade amounted to close to the majority of their total exports. When intra-regional trade is measured as a share of GCC GDP is also weak, particularly again when compared to the Eurozone countries prior to MU. The ratio of intra-regional exports to GDP in the Eurozone countries in 1998 was 12.8 per cent (Bayoumi and Mauro 1999) whereas in the GCC in 2006 the ratio was just 2.7 per cent (IMF 2007a, 2007b).

Historically, GCC states' similar trade structures meant that there have been few trading complementarities between them and consequently absolute trade flows between GCC states have been minimal.

However, we must be careful in drawing conclusions from the intra-GCC trade data as a share of total trade (including crude oil) which can be very misleading because of the distorting effect of oil prices. The share of intra-GCC trade as a proportion of total trade is very much dependent on the price of oil and during times of high oil prices the proportion of intra-GCC trade (which is predominantly non-crude oil trade) will inevitably fall and vice versa. The strong inverse relationship between intra-GCC trade and the oil price is illustrated in Figure 3.1, although in what may be a positive sign the share of intra-regional trade has remained stable in recent years despite oil prices rising markedly since 2002.

In the context of the GCC we consider it more meaningful therefore, to examine the share of intra-GCC *non-crude oil trade* as a proportion of GCC *non-oil GDP* and *total non-crude oil trade*. Measured in this way intra-GCC trade as a share of non-oil GDP doubles to 4.3 per cent for the region (see Figure 3.2). For individual GCC states this measure of their intra-regional trade interdependence can be much higher, for example in Bahrain and Oman it is above ten per cent and, perhaps surprisingly, for Qatar it is close to eight per cent.

Again, when intra-GCC *non-crude oil* exports are calculated as a share of total *non-crude oil* exports the level of trade intensity triples. In 2003 intra-GCC non-crude oil exports as a share of total non-crude oil exports constituted 16.3 per cent (see Table 3.1). Since 2000 intra-GCC non-crude oil exports formed on average 17 per cent of total non-crude oil trade. The value of intra-GCC non-crude oil exports also grew strongly by an annual growth rate of 10.1 per cent between 1990 and 2003. Furthermore, if crude oil *and* refined oil products are excluded then the intra-GCC share is all the more impressive and increases to more than a third of their total exports (Jadresic 2002: 10).[1] Therefore if we

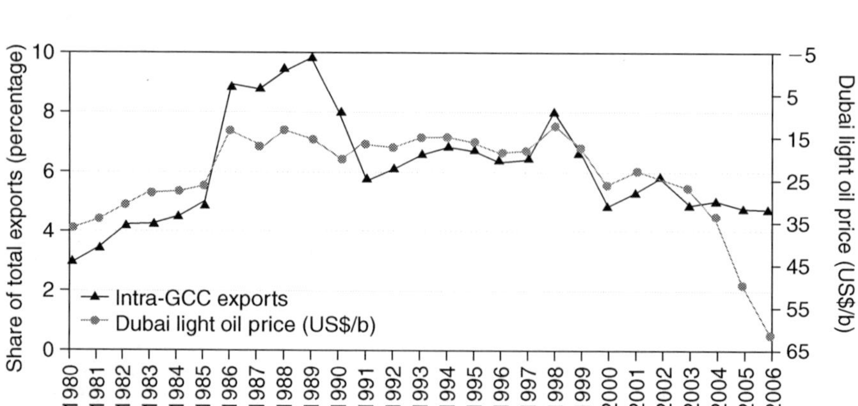

Figure 3.1 Intra-GCC exports and (inverted) crude oil prices, 1980–2006 (sources: Author's calculations based on data from IEA (2007); IMF (2007b)).

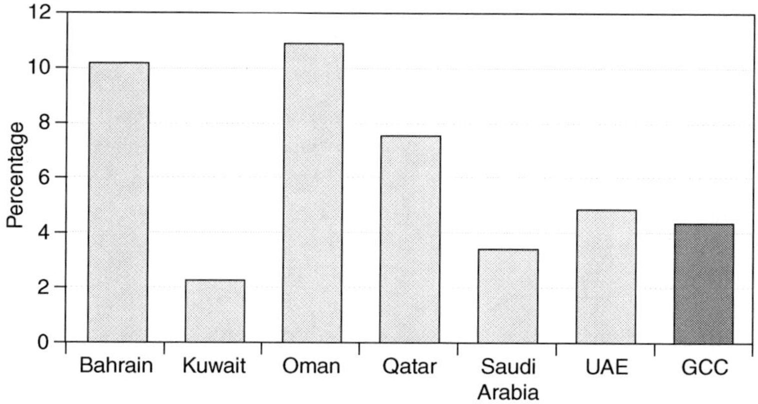

Figure 3.2 Non-oil intra-GCC trade as share of non-oil GDP, 2003 (sources: Author's calculations based on data from AMF (2006) and ESCWA (2007)).

Note: Oman figure is for 2002.

Table 3.1 Intra-GCC non-crude oil trade (per cent), selected years

		1990 (%)	*1995 (%)*	*2000 (%)*	*2001 (%)*	*2002 (%)*	*2003 (%)*
Bahrain	Exports	28.8	21.4	25.0	27.5	29.7	37.5
	Imports	9.5	13.3	14.7	14.4	15.0	16.1
Kuwait	Exports	28.3	3.8	3.7	5.5	5.4	5.4
	Imports	6.8	9.7	11.5	11.2	11.0	11.4
Oman	Exports	56.8	50.4	51.7	47.0	49.5	50.9
	Imports	27.0	28.7	33.2	33.2	33.2	27.8
Qatar	Exports	29.6	18.1	13.2	8.3	13.1	9.7
	Imports	8.6	10.2	14.9	12.2	15.4	14.9
KSA	Exports	11.6	25.5	16.5	15.0	17.4	20.0
	Imports	1.8	2.7	3.6	3.9	4.6	4.4
UAE	Exports	34.7	32.2	21.9	19.9	20.2	15.8
	Imports	6.3	5.0	4.5	4.8	5.4	5.0
GCC	Exports	16.9	16.9	16.8	16.1	18.1	16.3
	Imports	5.4	6.6	7.5	7.7	8.4	7.8

Source: Author's calculations based on data from ESCWA (2007 and various issues).

exclude crude oil and refined oil products, intra-GCC trade is more significant than often assumed, indeed it is a similar level to that of intra-ASEAN trade (Rana 2007: 714).

There are nevertheless significant disparities between the GCC states in terms of their regional trade integration. For Bahrain and Oman intra-GCC non-crude oil exports are considerably higher than for the bloc as a whole, where they formed 38 and 51 per cent of total non-oil exports respectively in 2003 (see Table 3.1).

An analysis of trade intensity ratios (TIR) also sheds light on the strength of intra-regional trade linkages between the GCC states. This ratio measures the strength of bilateral trade between two states in relation to one particular GCC country's trade with the world. It is specifically defined as the share of one country's exports going to a partner divided by the share of world exports going to that partner.[2] It can help to determine whether the value of trade between two countries is larger, or smaller, than would be expected given each country's share of world trade (however, again we must be aware that this measure of trade intensity will also be skewed by the oil price).

Nevertheless, this analysis reveals that with the exception of Kuwait and Saudi Arabia, the trade intensity ratios between the GCC states are always greater than one, implying a stronger bilateral trade flow than would otherwise be expected. Yet this ratio is also distorted by oil prices, falling when oil prices rise and vice versa, for the region as a whole the ratio stood at 0.58 in 2006, 0.82 in 2000 and 1.24 in 1990 when the oil price was much lower. On a bilateral level, the results indicate that the trade intensity ratios between Saudi Arabia and Bahrain and between the UAE and Oman are much greater than expected; both pairs of countries are in close geographical proximity and have land border crossings (see Table 3.2).[3]

In 2006 the Saudi–Bahrain TIR amounted to 30, this indicates that Saudi exports to Bahrain are particularly sizable in relation to the share of world exports destined for Bahrain and suggests that Saudi exports are particularly important for Bahrain. In fact, most of the Saudi exports destined for Bahrain is crude oil. Bahrain was the first GCC state to face the depletion of its oil reserves and dwindling oil production and began importing significant volumes of discounted crude oil from Saudi Arabia, which are then exported as petroleum products from the Sitra refinery.

In 2006 the UAE's TIR with Oman was also very high at 24, compared to an average of two with its other GCC neighbours (see Table 3.2). The UAE and Oman have shared borders and are geographically interlinked which has undoubtedly fostered a close commercial relationship. Moreover the UAE is a

Table 3.2 GCC trade intensity ratios, 2006

	Bahrain	*Kuwait*	*Oman*	*Qatar*	*Saudi Arabia*	*UAE*
Bahrain	–	5.25	13.97	4.68	6.06	2.62
Kuwait	1.30	–	1.55	0.80	1.09	0.80
Oman	2.59	2.75	–	2.25	2.12	7.18
Qatar	2.33	2.87	1.43	–	0.77	3.27
Saudi Arabia	30.06	4.33	2.22	0.12	–	1.35
UAE	3.68	3.75	23.77	4.03	2.86	–

Source: Calculated from IMF (2007b).

Note
Exporters are in left-hand column and importers across the top.

major re-export hub for the Gulf region with strong exports to other GCC states; non-oil intra-GCC exports accounted on average for a fifth of the UAE's total non-oil exports since 2000. Only Kuwait and to a lesser extent Qatar have relatively weak trade intensity ratios (see Table 3.2). However, the TIR between the GCC's two largest economies, Saudi Arabia and the UAE, is also very weak.

Findings from the GCC business survey also indicate that intra-regional trade is perhaps relatively more significant than conventionally assumed. Of the business respondents, a majority – 58 per cent – stated that they had some involvement in foreign trade. When these respondents were asked about the extent of their involvement in intra-GCC trade, more than two-thirds said that the region they exported to most was the GCC. Furthermore, the majority of those businesses that said they exported most to the GCC were small and medium sized enterprises (SMEs) – 84 per cent having less than 250 employees and 82 per cent having less than $50 million annual turnover.[4] It is generally considered to be the case that SMEs form the greatest part of the GCC business community and therefore it is important that these businesses are also significantly involved in intra-regional trade.[5]

So far this analysis of trade has been static, concentrating on the past, yet the trading relations between GCC states are dynamic and historical patterns are not necessarily a reliable guide to future trade intensity. Therefore it is important that we should now focus on the prospects for intra-GCC trade growing in the coming period. Two areas where increasing opportunities for intra-GCC trade are appearing are in intra-industry trade and energy trade. In recent years there has been increasing investment and intra-GCC competition in downstream hydrocarbon-related activities including refining, petrochemicals and the manufacture of basic metals. There are now substantial investments taking place in these sectors across the bloc. The GCC transitional economies are still developing and as they do so their industrial structure should become more specialized, research has shown that the more advanced and developed an economy, the greater will be its degree of industrial specialization (Grubel and Lloyd 1975). In the future, as these industries mature and specialization takes place there should be increasing opportunities for intra-industry trade between the GCC states.

Intra-GCC energy trade is also set to grow considerably. Qatar is already supplying natural gas to the UAE and Oman while Bahrain and Kuwait are also seeking deals to import Qatari gas for use in domestic electricity generation and as feedstock for petrochemical production. Bahrain and Oman will also need to import more oil and gas in the coming decades as their resources deplete – sourcing this at competitive prices from their GCC neighbours.

In summary, the balance of evidence indicates that intra-GCC trade is somewhat more significant and important than often thought (particularly for the region's SMEs) and there are also signs that intra-GCC trade is likely to grow in the future. Our analysis has also shown that intra-GCC trade is more significant for some GCC states, e.g. Bahrain, Oman, and the UAE, than for the others, which will have implications for the distribution of costs and benefits resulting from the MU project (see Chapter 7). In particular, the weakness of trade linkages between Saudi Arabia and the UAE, the two largest GCC economies, is an issue to which we will return to later on in this chapter. Nevertheless, at this juncture and from a static sense, the GCC do not meet this OCA criterion.

Labour market mobility

GCC labour markets can be characterized by their highly segmented nature; in fact, there are two distinct labour markets within each GCC state: the national and the expatriate labour force. Both groups exhibit very different degrees of mobility and wage flexibility. A high degree of labour market mobility between the member states of an MU is important because without flexible exchange rates (and concomitantly independent interest rate setting) to offset asymmetric economic shocks the onus will be on national labour markets and wages to adjust in order to maintain full employment. While the contention holds that the more mobile labour is within an economic region the better suited it is to MU, evidence from the Eurozone illustrates that relatively low levels of labour mobility in itself is not a barrier to establishing MU (Soltwedel *et al.* 1999).

The expatriate labour force

The majority of the GCC labour force – 62 per cent on aggregate – is expatriate; this share ranges from a low of 49.5 per cent of the total labour force in Saudi Arabia to a high of 90 per cent in the UAE (see Table 3.3). The expatriate labour force is, by its very nature, inherently mobile. A large pool of labour exists predominantly in South and South East Asia, which is relatively cheap as it is available at international prices and is also highly elastic. During the ongoing oil price boom wages in the private sector have not risen at anywhere near the rate of inflation in the goods and asset markets, indicating a high degree of labour market mobility and flexibility.

Table 3.3 Composition of GCC labour force (per cent)

	Total labour force		*Public sector*		*Private sector*	
	National	*Expatriate*	*National*	*Expatriate*	*National*	*Expatriate*
Bahrain	36.1	63.9	90.8	9.2	28.6	72.4
Kuwait	16.9	83.1	74.6	25.4	2.7	97.3
Oman	28.7	71.3	80.5	19.5	15.5	84.5
Qatar	44.8	55.2	52.8	47.2	17.0	83.0
KSA	50.5	49.5	91.3	8.7	45.3	54.7
UAE	10.4	89.6	27.4	72.6	1.3	98.7
GCC	38.3	61.7	72.3	27.7	31.7	68.3

Source: Author's calculations based on a range of national data sources.

Note
The range of data used spans 2002–2006.

The vast majority of expatriate workers are employed in the private sector, accounting for more than two-thirds of the private sector labour force (see Table 3.3). The region's private sector has undoubtedly benefited from this cheap and flexible supply of expatriate labour, which has a low reservation wage, can be employed on short-term fixed contracts, work long hours and is easy to hire and fire. This is reflected in the World Bank Rigidity of Employment Index, which averages at 25 for the GCC states – significantly less than that of the Eurozone countries at 48 (World Bank 2007b). Employment legislation in the GCC states is considered to be very relaxed in relation to expatriate labour, trade unions are illegal in most GCC states and there is no minimum wage.

Following an economic shock, whether affecting the region's economies symmetrically or asymmetrically, immigrant labour flows respond quickly and therefore cyclical unemployment in the private sector has not been a problem for the GCC states. In the case of a negative asymmetric national shock, despite legal restrictions preventing expatriate labour from moving directly from one GCC state to another, immigrant labour will respond first by returning to their countries of origin and then re-emigrating to another GCC state.

The national labour force

Despite governments enacting legislative reforms to remove legal barriers to the intra-GCC movement of national labour, this cohort is, in contrast to that of expatriates, considered to be very rigid. Articles Eight and Nine of the 1981 Economic Agreement allowed for the equal treatment of GCC citizens with regard to freedom of work, residence, ownership, inheritance and undertaking economic activities across the member states (GCC Secretariat 1981). The 2001 Economic Agreement went much further, taking steps to remove economic disincentives to intra-regional labour mobility. Article Three accorded the equal treatment of GCC citizens in both the private and public sectors as well as in terms of pensions, social security, and health and education provision (GCC Secretariat General 2001).

At the 2004 GCC summit the region's leaders agreed to extend social security and civil service retirement to those GCC nationals working in other GCC states, irrespective of whether they work in the public sector or the private sector. A deadline for 2010 was set for completing a unified system which would guarantee all GCC nationals their pension and social security.

Despite the legal freedom to work in other GCC states, there is little hard evidence to suggest any significant intra-GCC national labour mobility exists at present. Figures on intra-GCC national labour flows have not been systematically collected up until now – probably because of the limited movements. Recently the GCC Public Social Insurance Authorities have begun collecting this data in preparation for the move towards extending social security and pension provision to those GCC nationals working in other member states (Badr-El-Din 2005: 17).

Despite a shared language and many other shared traits a combination of cultural and socio-economic factors impedes the intra-regional mobility of the GCC national labour force. In part, cultural characteristics such as a strong familial ties and significant family responsibilities play an important role. In a survey of Saudi youths from the Al Hassa region of Eastern Province in Saudi Arabia, over 90 per cent wanted to work locally and few were prepared to contemplate relocation to obtain work (Bosbait and Wilson 2005). Relocating to work in another GCC state may also mean missing out on benefits only available to nationals residing in their own country such as land grants, subsidized building loans and marriage grants.

Not only do national labour force rigidities manifest themselves in the low levels of intra-regional labour flows but also in the limited mobility of nationals between the private and public sectors within any given state. Traditionally, the public sector has been the principal employer of nationals and still today nationals account for on average 72 per cent of the public sector labour force (see Table 3.3). In several GCC states the right to employment was enshrined in legislation and translated into guaranteed public sector jobs for nationals (Sassanpour *et al.* 1997). The popularity of the public sector stems from the fact that it generally provides salaries and other benefits at a premium to that on offer in the private sector, consequently the reservation wage of nationals is often far too high for many private sector job openings (Sassanpour *et al.* 1997).

However, expectations about obtaining a public sector position have become increasingly unrealistic. Years of strong population growth have generated an expansive population pyramid where on average 28 per cent of the population, is now under the age of 15 compared with just 17 per cent in the EMU countries (see Figure 3.3). Consequently, new national entrants to the labour market have been estimated at 210,000 annually (Girgis 2002: 35). It is no longer fiscally sustainable or productive for the public sector to go on providing employment for all new national labour market entrants. As there is limited scope to further

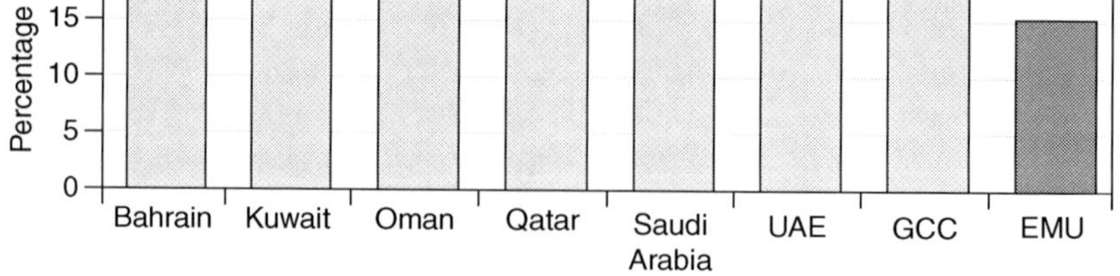

Figure 3.3 Share of GCC population below age of 15, 2005 (source: World Bank (2007a)).

national employment in the public sector governments are now looking at ways to 'encourage' their respective private sectors to help solve the national unemployment problem. This is being addressed either directly – by applying quotas and reserving some vocations for nationals alone or indirectly – by raising the cost of hiring expatriate labour.

The effect of labour nationalization policies

Such labour nationalization policies, if implemented too stringently on the private sector, may eventually erode the degree to which the GCC bloc meets this criterion. Furthermore, if policies are not harmonized some economies will become less competitive than others. At the 2001 GCC summit, all the GCC leaders agreed to a policy of reducing foreign workers gradually and setting quotas for national employment in the private sector as well as increasing taxes on expatriate recruitment through raising recruitment fees for expatriates and more severely enforcing immigration and labour laws (ESCWA 2003).

In short, many private sector businesses are against such policies, national labour is considered to be more expensive (Gulf nationals have a higher reservation wage thanks to well-remunerated jobs in the public sector) while their vocational skills and experience may not be on a par with like-for-like expatriate workers. Research by Al-Qudsi (2006) found that secondary school graduate expatriate workers in Kuwait, aged between 20 and 29, had on average, eight more years of experience and cost 135 per cent less than unemployed Kuwaitis fitting the same criteria.

In the short to medium term, it seems that the GCC economies will have little choice but to continue to rely on expatriate labour for the growth of the private sector it helps keep businesses internationally competitive and also keeps the labour market flexible. In the long run, however, those GCC states that provide their citizens with the best vocational education and split some of the benefits from public sector employment (such as providing pensions for all national employees regardless of whether they are employed in the public or private sector) will be best able to replace expatriates without incurring too much cost.

Capital market integration

The original OCA criteria did not specifically cover or consider the role of risk sharing, portfolio diversification or capital market integration, but a decade after setting out the original theory it was broadened to include these considerations (Mundell 1973). It was argued that a high degree of capital market integration would allow MU members to hold claims on each other's output, insuring themselves against asymmetric shocks. It follows that if one member were hit by an economic downturn the income from capital assets held in other member states not suffering from the negative shock, this would offset the decline in domestic income, allowing for consumption smoothing and limiting the economic damage.

While the shared dependence on oil may mean that GCC capital markets are likely to face similar shocks resulting from oil price changes on balance, the weight of research suggests that there are potential risk-sharing gains from regional portfolio diversification. Hammoudeh and Kyongwook (2004) found only weak correlation between the returns of the GCC markets and that country idiosyncrasies as well as the oil price influence stock returns. In addition, Bley and Chen (2006) also find evidence to support the role for risk sharing, with market return behavior in the GCC still 'far from homogeneous' (Bley and Chen 2006: 90).

Evidence from the Eurozone indicates that this criterion is also in part endogenous to the process of MU itself. Following the launch of the euro, Eurozone capital markets experienced much greater integration and benefited as a result (Bernanke 2004), something we will consider later on in Chapter 6 of this book. In our following analysis of GCC capital mobility, we will focus in particular on portfolio investment, banking and finally on intra-GCC FDI flows.

Intra-GCC portfolio investment and banking

Historically, much of the GCC's capital stock has been held outside of the region, particularly in US assets with little being invested in the region's capital markets. However, since 2000 several factors have combined leading to significant increases in regional capital retention and thus greater opportunities for intra-GCC portfolio diversification and capital market integration. In addition to the stimulus provided by the excess liquidity resulting from high oil prices and increased demand for assets, the stock market gains were also attributable to a new 'home bias' for investments following the terrorist attacks of 9/11 and the freezing of some Arab investments in the US as well as structural reforms taking place in the region (Al-Hassan *et al.* 2007).

Despite a significant correction in 2006, GCC stock market capitalization increased fivefold between the end of 2000 and the second quarter of 2007 with aggregate market capitalization growing from $117 billion to $716 billion (see Figure 3.4). The stellar performance of the GCC stock markets in recent years has encouraged widespread participation of Gulf nationals in stock trading attracted to the market by large potential gains. It was estimated that in Saudi Arabia more than 50 per cent of the entire population were investing in its stock market in 2005 (Ahmad 2005). The massive growth in market capitalization has also attracted increasing numbers of partial flotations of family owned and quasi-public sector entities. Between 2000 and 2007 market listings increased by 90 per cent – from 333 companies to 631 (see Figure 3.4). Recent stock market growth and increased regional participation have strengthened the potential role of risk sharing from intra-regional portfolio diversification which would be beneficial to the MU project.

Up until recently, GCC nationals were only allowed to trade and own shares in other member states in specified stocks, with the exception of the Kuwaiti and Bahraini markets which were fully open to GCC nationals (see Table 3.4). Since

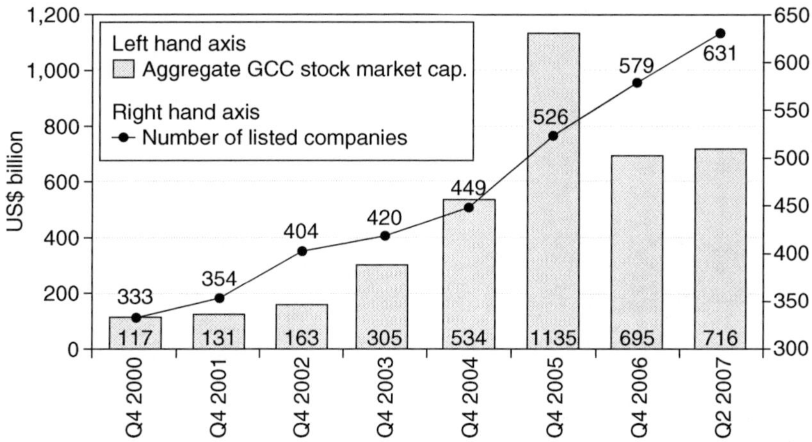

Figure 3.4 GCC stock market performance (source: Author's calculations based on data from AMF (2007 and various years)).

2005 steps have been taken to ratify Article Five of the 2001 Economic Agreement, in which the GCC states agreed to 'unify their investment-related laws and regulations, accord national treatment to all investments owned by GCC natural and legal citizens and integrate financial markets in member states, and unify all related legislation and policies' (GCC Secretariat General 2001: Article Five). Subsequently in late 2005 Saudi Arabia and the UAE also granted equal treatment of GCC citizens in trading on national stock markets and Qatar and Oman have also taken steps towards this (Abdul Ghafour 2005).

Despite legislating to allow nationals from other GCC states to invest in their capital markets, it is difficult to assess empirically the actual degree of intra-regional portfolio investment because of incomplete data on intra-GCC portfolio flows. Yet there is much anecdotal evidence of increased appetite for regional investments. There are numerous GCC-wide investment funds now available to GCC investors looking to diversify risks across the bloc, such as mutual funds including equities, fixed income, property, hedge funds and Islamically compliant funds provided by both national and international banks. By early 2007 the Abu Dhabi Stock Market (ADSM) reportedly had 54,000 registered Omani investors – 7 per cent of the total registered investors on the exchange and in addition foreign investor activity on the ADSM – the bulk of which is likely to be GCC nationals (given restrictions on foreign investors) – is currently estimated to account for 10 per cent on the market's turnover (*Executive Magazine* 2007). In Bahrain, where participation has been open to all GCC nationals since 1999, the majority of Bahraini listed company shares – 54 per cent – were owned by other GCC nationals in 2005 up from 43 per cent in 2000 (Bahrain Monetary Agency 2007). In 2005 newspapers reported that 'plane loads of Saudis' descended on the UAE in a rush to subscribe for the IPO of Dana Gas, 'creating a virtual stampede in receiving banks' (Carvalho 2005).

Table 3.4 GCC citizens' access to listed companies on national stock markets

Stock markets	*Bahrain*	*Kuwait*	*Oman*	*Qatar*	*KSA*	*UAE*	*GCC*
							1985
No. of stock companies	23	33	24	10	43	37	170
Open to GCC nationals	16	1	6	–	3	16	42
Per cent of companies	70%	3%	25%	–	7%	43%	25%
							1995
No. of stock companies	34	41	75	29	88	76	343
Open to GCC nationals	34	41	66	3	75	34	254
Per cent of companies	100%	100%	88%	10%	85%	45%	74%
							2005
No. of stock companies	47	156	127[a]	36[b]	77	89	532
Open to GCC nationals	47	156	121[a]	32[b]	77	89	522
Per cent of companies	100%	100%	95%	88%	100%	100%	98%

Source: Adapted by author from GCC Secretariat General (2006); national stock market data (accessed 2007).

Notes
a 2006
b 2003.
At the 2002 GCC summit all states agreed to work towards fully opening their respective stock markets to GCC nationals.

Another indicator of capital market integration within the region is the number of company cross-listings on the markets. A substantial and increasing number of cross-listings within the GCC would be indicative of significant integration between the region's bourses and the regional orientation of GCC companies. However, cross-border listings of companies on GCC stock markets in 2005 was relatively low at just 4 per cent of the total companies listed on the GCC bourses (see Table 3.5). Despite this, the number of cross-listings has grown substantially by an annual growth rate of 47 per cent since 2000.

In terms of institutional and regulatory coordination of the region's stock markets there has been more limited progress to date. GCC states have different regulatory frameworks imposing transaction costs and hindering the flow of capital between markets. Yet the harmonization of the regulatory and supervisory frameworks is essential for greater integration and would be most cost effective if undertaken by a pan-GCC regional regulatory authority. This is a major objective of building a GCC common market (as laid out in Article Five of the 2001 Economic Agreement) but as yet it appears few steps have been taken to achieve a harmonization of GCC financial market regulations and supervision.

Turning to GCC bond markets, historically these have been rather underdeveloped and there is ample room for expansion, yet this is rapidly changing. Interest in Islamic finance – in particular Islamic bonds or *sukuks* – has increased markedly in the past few years and the GCC is fast overtaking Kuala

Table 3.5 Growth of GCC stock market cross-listings

Market	*2000*	*2001*	*2002*	*2003*	*2004*	*2005*
Bahrain						
Bahrain Stock Exchange	2	3	4	4	6	8
Kuwait						
Kuwait Stock Exchange	0	0	0	1	1	2
UAE						
Abu Dhabi Securities Market	0	0	1	3	3	6
UAE						
Dubai Financial Market	0	0	1	1	2	4
Total	2	3	6	9	12	20
Annual growth	–	50%	100%	50%	33%	67%

Source: Calculated by author from Issa (2006).

Lumpur in becoming the global centre for issuance and also secondary trading. GCC companies and governments issued over $11 billion in Islamic bonds between 2001 and 2006 and there is increasing integration and cooperation on issuance between institutions across the GCC states (McSheehy 2006).

For example, the Sokouk Holding Company, based in Kuwait and its partners, including Kuwait Investment and Qatar Islamic Bank, plan to spend $200 million setting up an Islamic Bond Exchange Centre in Bahrain (McSheehy 2006). Bahrain, Kuwait, Saudi Arabia and the UAE have already collaborated in establishing an award winning Liquidity Management Center in Bahrain which facilitates investment of surplus funds from Islamic banks and financial institutions into short- and medium term financial instruments in accordance with the Sharia principles.[6]

Up until recently integration of the region's retail banking sectors has been limited with only a few banks opening operations in neighbouring states. Since 1980 very few licences were granted for new banks across the GCC. National banks were largely protected from regional and international competition by strong legal constraints that have allowed them to earn huge economic rents. At the 1997 GCC summit however the GCC leaders agreed to open up their banking sectors to each other and to establish the Gulf Network of the National Automated Teller Machines. By 2004 under pressure from WTO agreements the banking sector across the GCC was opening up gradually to both international and regional competition. According to Wilson (2004), by 2004 the National Bank of Kuwait, Emirates International Bank and the Bahrain-based Gulf International Bank had all opened branches in Riyadh.[7] At present the GCC Secretariat is working towards establishing an integrated payments system across the bloc by 2010. Such a system will allow GCC nationals to conduct their banking activities in any GCC state and facilitate cross-border payments between businesses.

Intra-GCC foreign direct investment

In the past, intra-GCC FDI flows have been minimal. According to available estimates, between 1990 and 2003, total intra-GCC FDI amounted to $3.6 billion, whereas aggregate GCC outflows reached approximately $125 billion over the same period, thus intra-GCC FDI formed only 2.9 per cent of total FDI attributable to GCC nationals (Bolbol and Fatheldin 2006). The region's two largest economies, Saudi Arabia and the UAE, received the major shares of intra-GCC FDI, at 54.2 per cent and 23.4 per cent respectively, while Kuwait's share was negligible and Oman's only amounted to 1.7 per cent of the total (Bolbol and Fatheldin 2006).

However, since 2003 when the last official figures became available, a far larger amount of the surplus oil revenues than previous has been retained and reinvested within the region. Not only has this resulted in high levels of GDP growth across the Gulf and boosted private sector confidence, but it has also led to increasing levels of intra-GCC FDI flows. Much of the evidence is anecdotal and has yet to feed into national or regional statistics which are untimely but the phenomenon is widespread and well documented in the region and indicates that the level of intra-GCC FDI throughout the 1990s has been dwarfed since the start of the current oil price boom.

According the Saudi Arabian General Investment Authority (SAGIA) the UAE has overtaken Japan as the main source of FDI into Saudi Arabia (*Gulf News* 2006). For example, in 2004 the UAE's state-owned telecommunications company, Etisalat, was the lead member of a consortium – Ettihad Etisalat – which won the licence to operate Saudi Arabia's second GSM network, in a bid estimated to be worth $3.2 billion (Reuters News Agency 2004). More recently, and by far the most noteworthy instance of intra-regional investment to date, was the Emirati company Emaar's $26 billion investment in the recently launched Saudi Arabian 'King Abdullah Economic City' (*Middle East Economic Digest* 2006). In mid-2006 SAGIA announced plans for another economic city, the $8 billion 'Prince Abdul Aziz Bin Musaid Economic City'. Many GCC entities have already committed to invest in the City including the UAE's Abu Dhabi Investment Authority, Abu Dhabi Investment House, Bahrain's Gulf Finance House and the Kuwaiti Investment Company and General Warehousing Company (Carvalho 2006).

Saudi Arabia is reciprocating and investing considerable sums into the UAE. For instance, Al Hanoo Holding Company is developing two major projects, the tourist-orientated $4.9 billion 'Nujoom Islands' and the $800 million 'Emirates Industrial City', both in the Emirate of Sharjah, and Saudi Oger is funding a $500 million real estate project 'Saraya Islands' in the Emirate of Ras Al Khaimah. Yet another Saudi company, Al Rajhi Group, has a 38.5 per cent stake in the $8.2 billion, 'Al Salam City' megaproject, taking shape in the Emirate of Umm Al Quwain (AMEinfo 2005). Saudi Arabia's Savola Group plans to open six HyperPanda retail outlets in the UAE at an estimated cost of $82 billion; the group's first foreign retail expansion (AMEinfo 2006b).

If it continues this cross-border investment should increase the economic interdependence between these states for example by holding claims on Saudi Arabia's economic output the UAE could mitigate the potential effects of future national shocks. This may prove to be a useful hedge against asymmetric shocks for the UAE and the smaller GCC states given that Saudi Arabia is likely to have considerable influence within the MU.

Economic diversification

The idea that the more economically diversified potential member economies are, the more suited they will be for MU, was developed by Kenen (1969). He argued that if prospective members had diversified economic structures they would be less likely to suffer from asymmetric shocks which might otherwise require the use of national monetary policies.

In the GCC economic dependency ratios clearly illustrate a fundamental common economic dependency on hydrocarbon resources; on average since 1991 oil and gas income constituted 35 per cent of GDP, 77 per cent of total exports and 74 per cent of government revenues.[8] It was shown in Chapter 2 that the composition of the GCC economies has remained relatively unchanged over the last decade with oil and gas constituting the single largest sector in terms of its contribution to economic activity. There are however, varying degrees of oil dependency among the GCC states, as illustrated in Figure 3.5. Nevertheless, even those countries with relatively lower oil dependencies, such as Bahrain and the UAE, remain unquestionably dominated by the hydrocarbons compared with any other grouping of world economies. Without wanting to detract from regional success stories, such as Bahrain and the UAE, the banking and finance

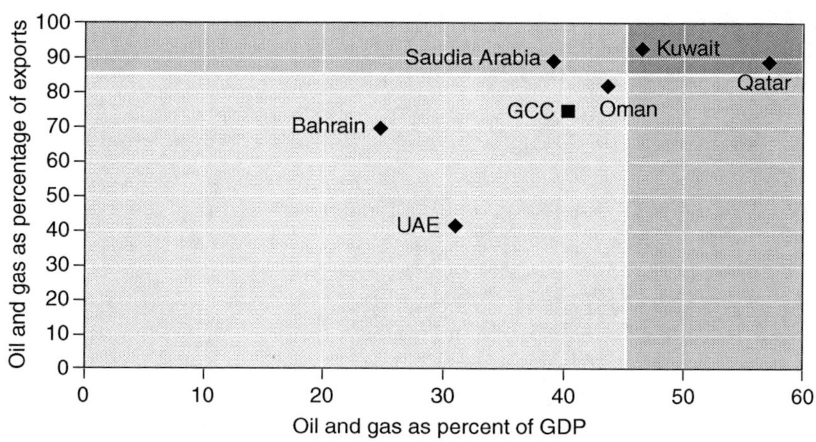

Figure 3.5 GCC oil dependency (sources: Author's calculations based on data from AMF (2006 and various years) and various GCC central bank reports).

Note
The figures are average dependencies based on data from the years 2001 to 2005.

as well as tourism sectors of their economies undoubtedly benefit from the increased regional liquidity during times of high oil prices (see Chapter 2).

However this failure to significantly diversify away from oil and gas does not in itself mean that MU would be inappropriate. Of course, diversification away from oil and gas may be desirable for a number of reasons, in particular employment creation and increased economic stability, but it is not necessarily an obstacle to MU. The similarity of economic structures and shared oil dependence implies that an oil price shock should affect *all the GCC states*, albeit to varying degrees, and as such, it could be addressed with a common monetary policy without causing problems for any individual member state.

In short, as long as the GCC states remain undiversified – but *undiversified in the same manner* – this does not necessarily mean they are unsuitable for an MU. What is really important is that, as they diversify away from oil and gas they do so without becoming overly specialized in any one particular industry into which they diversify.

At this point it will be useful to make a conceptual distinction in terms of the type of diversification required for MU. The MU project requires that the GCC move towards greater *within country* diversification rather than *within region* diversification. Within country diversification is where each country in a regional grouping contemplating MU becomes internally diversified (i.e. has a wide range of different industries and services). Clearly, where all the countries in the potential MU are diversified in this manner then the problem of an asymmetric shock will not be particularly problematic for the MU. Each of the countries in the region with a diversified portfolio of industries will experience the specific shock in a similar manner and to a similar degree. Therefore an MU and a common monetary policy will be appropriate for all of them or, to put it the other way round, none of them will feel obliged to break away and adopt an independent monetary policy to deal with that particular asymmetric shock.

It has been argued by some economists (for example see Sturm and Siegfried 2005: 19) that with greater economic diversification the GCC economies will become more heterogeneous and more vulnerable to asymmetric shocks. Consequently, an aggregate monetary policy based on the economic circumstances of the entire region will be less likely to be optimal for each member state. However, this particular argument would only apply where the diversification in question is what we have called *within region* diversification i.e. where the different countries in the potential MU diversify away from a common, predominant industry (in the GCC case, oil), but do so by each country becoming specialized in a different industry. In other words if one country 'diversifies' by becoming *specialized* in aluminium production for example, another in tourism, another in financial services etc. then this kind of heterogeneity would certainly leave them vulnerable to asymmetric shocks and make an MU and common monetary policy inappropriate for them as a group.

This also means that some of those regional commentators who have expressed concern about the different GCC countries diversifying into the same industries and services and therefore competing with each other may be failing to recognize that a diversification strategy which involves some replication of new industries and services around the Gulf is not just beneficial in stimulating intra-regional competition but also beneficial to the MU project.[9]

Where diversification away from hydrocarbons *is* occurring there are some hopeful signs that the dangers of specialization i.e. *within region* diversification, are being avoided and that *within country* diversification is, indeed, beginning to take place. The fact that the GCC states have similar comparative advantages means that economic diversification is taking place in the same sectors and industries which should lessen the potential for them to be hit by asymmetric shocks. In particular two areas where significant diversification is taking place is in the downstream petroleum industry and the service sector.

There is undoubtedly prolific anecdotal evidence of intra-GCC competition taking place within downstream heavy industry and the service sectors. With increased regional competition greater industrial and service sector specialization should eventually take place as these sectors mature leading to greater intra-industry and intra-service trading opportunities which should be bolstered by a single currency. Since the start of the current oil price boom, according to *Middle East Economic Digest* an estimated $106 billion worth of petrochemical projects had been announced across the GCC, $44 billion worth of industrial projects and more than $400 billion worth of construction projects – where substantial new building of hotels and tourist attractions is taking place (AMEinfo 2006a).

All of the GCC states have moved away from the simple extraction of crude oil and natural gas to downstream activities. This 'vertical' diversification into associated or 'value-added' hydrocarbon products has focused not just on the refining of crude oil but also in the development of the petrochemical industry, chemical fertilizers and manufacture of basic metals. The GCC refining industry is currently witnessing an upsurge in growth with several GCC states now investing in new refining capacity and new petrochemical complexes are also being constructed throughout the GCC. Aluminium smelting is another key industry where substantial capacity expansion is taking place within the region. New smelters or expansions of existing plants are in the pipeline in every GCC state with the exception of Kuwait.

In particular there are two areas of tertiary sector activity where intra-GCC competition is strong: banking and finance and tourism. Banking and finance has benefited from the tax-free nature of the Gulf and tourism has grown substantially in liberal states, taking advantage from the warm winter climate and considerable investment in tourist facilities.

Bahrain has the longest established financial centre in the Gulf but is facing increasing regional competition from Dubai and Qatar's emerging financial centres. All three states are building new financial centres and are competing to become the 'GCC financial capital', the new financial hub for the Middle East and emerging markets. Bahrain is constructing a new $1.3 billion financial centre – the 'Bahrain Financial Harbour' – the Qatar Financial Centre was launched in January 2005 and the UAE has established the Dubai International

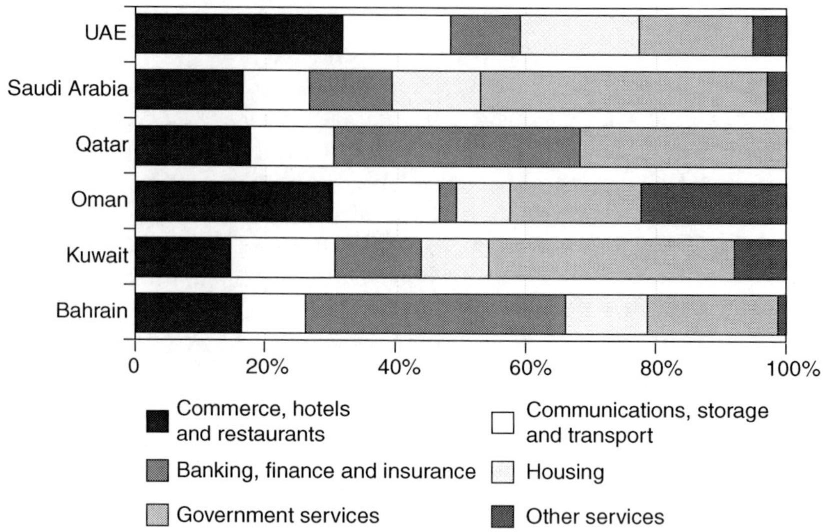

Figure 3.6 Breakdown of GCC service sectors, 2005 (sources: Author's calculations based on AMF data from (2006 and various years); Bahrain Monetary Agency (2007) data).

Financial Centre. Currently banking and finance forms the largest part of the service sector in both Bahrain and Qatar at approximately 40 and 41 per cent of their service sector activities respectively (see Figure 3.6). Saudi Arabia is also hoping to develop its financial services sector, in the pipeline is the 'Financial Island' district of the 'King Abdullah Economic City'. Intra-GCC competition in financial services should improve the sector's performance across the GCC and could also lead to increasing intra-service sector trade.

Tourism is an area where Oman and the UAE are competing but they are not the only GCC states targeting this sector for growth, Bahrain and Qatar are too. In Oman and the UAE, tourism accounts for the largest share – at 30 and 32 per cent respectively – of their total service sector activities (see Figure 3.6). As of 2004, Dubai had 272 hotels, 30 shopping malls and almost 5 million foreign visitors (*The Economist* 2004) and by 2015, Dubai alone hopes to attract 15 million tourists annually (Wallis 2005). While Oman cannot compete with the shopping malls of Dubai in the UAE, it has a diverse natural environment which will attract a different niche of visitors. In June 2005, Oman unveiled the $15 billion 'Blue City' tourist development to be built in the coastal region at Al-Sawaidi. This massive economic development project will include hotels, apartments, leisure and healthcare facilities. Other tourist-related projects include the $805 million 'The Wave' development, which has successfully attracted significant levels of FDI.

Bahrain has long been a favoured destination for GCC tourists and is doing everything it can to maintain this position and compete with the newer hot-spots offered by Dubai and Muscat. It is building a string of new resorts and five-star hotels and on top of the causeway linking the island state with Saudi Arabia is planning one with Qatar. In addition, it hosts the only Formula One race to take place in the Middle East. Qatar, not content with its newly established financial centre and educational zones that have attracted various US and British universities, is also expanding into tourism. It recently hosted the Asian Games and like most of the other GCC states is building a wide range of tourist facilities such as the Qatar Pearl – a string of reclaimed islands with yachting facilities and numerous international hotels.

Economic synchronization

The final criterion we are covering in this study, which has also been the subject of much empirical testing, is the degree of economic synchronization between the GCC states, i.e. are their respective business cycles moving together on a long-run path. The prospective member economies will be fully synchronized when they are facing symmetric economic shocks and when they respond and adjust symmetrically to those shocks. According to the traditional OCA theory, if the economies of the prospective member states are not synchronized i.e. they face asymmetric shocks and/or respond asymmetrically then they are less likely to be suited to MU because they will be on diverging economic paths that would be best managed using independent interest rate setting rather than a common monetary policy (Mundell 1961).

On the one hand, the similar structure of the GCC economies (see previous section) has led many experts to assume that their economies are synchronized and experience symmetric economic shocks, mainly stemming from changes in the oil price. However, the fact that the GCC economies are not homogenous and have achieved various degrees of diversification (see Figure 3.5) is likely to effect the extent to which they are synchronized and their response to a common oil price shock. Another factor which will have a bearing on the degree of economic synchronization is the degree to which these countries are integrated through trade. According to Frankel and Rose (1997) the greater the degree of trade intensity between a group of countries the higher the degree of economic synchronization.

In the case of EMU there has been much empirical work on economic shock synchronization. The results have suggested that, prior to MU, the European economies were not all ideal candidates for MU. For example, Bayoumi and Eichengreen (1992) found that shocks to output and prices were significantly more idiosyncratic across the European member states than across US states. In addition, the authors' research suggested that there may be a 'two-speed' Europe in that supply and demand shocks to a 'core' group of European countries were closely correlated compared to the shocks facing the 'periphery' countries which were less correlated.

To date, only a few research papers have employed econometric techniques in order to examine the synchronization of the GCC economies, however as we shall see, the results of existing research illustrates that in general the GCC states can be considered economically synchronized reasonably well but that there appear to be some notable national deviations.

Research by Laabas and Limam (2002) establishes long-run synchronization between the GCC economies but their analysis also revealed some national disparities in the degree of synchronization. The authors analyze the synchronicity of the GCC economies by examining their real exchange rates which are considered to reflect underlying macroeconomic variables. Laabas and Limam conclude that overall the GCC real exchange rates share the same trend with the caveat that their results illustrated national differences. The results for Oman and the UAE indicated a slower speed of adjustment towards the long-run relationship and therefore a different response to an oil price shock. According to the authors: 'Oman is the least favourable candidate for currency union' (Laabas and Limam 2002: 24), they also contend that 'Oman and (the) UAE may be considered a less homogeneous subset than the rest of (the) GCC countries for the constitution of a currency union' (Laabas and Limam 2002: 24). In conclusion the authors contend that greater policy coordination and synchronization is required for the GCC MU to be successful (see Table 3.6).

A study by Darrat and Al-Shamsi (2005) finds evidence of a long-run common trend in five economic variables of the GCC states: real GDP, inflation rates, exchange rates, money stock and the money base (see Table 3.6). Following an economic shock, short-run divergences may occur but eventually these economies will adjust and return to a long-run equilibrium path. Darrat and Al-Shamsi (2005) acknowledge however that their methodology is somewhat limited in that it cannot shed light on the short-run dynamics or the relationship or the degree of integration on a state-by-state basis. In conclusion the authors

Table 3.6 Selected research testing for GCC economic synchronization

Econometric research by	*Methodology*	*Data period*	*Collective synchronization*	*National disparities*
Kamar and Ben Naceur (2007)	Pooled mean group using panel data	1992–2005	Yes	Yes, Oman and UAE
Rutledge (2007)	Bilateral cointegration between Saudi Arabia and rest of GCC	1981–2004	Yes	Yes, Kuwait and the UAE
Darrat and Al-Shamsi (2005)	Multi-cointegration of five economic variables	1971–2001	Yes	No testing
Laabas and Limam (2002)	Cointegration of real exchange rates	1960–1999	Yes	Yes, Oman and the UAE

Source: Compiled by author.

argue that there are no economic obstacles to increasing GCC economic integration and that the impediments that have stalled the process so far must be 'sociopolitical factors' (Darrat and Al-Shamsi 2005: 1061).

An IMF working paper by Kamar and Ben Naceur (2007) also models the real exchange rates of the GCC. This time the authors examine the common economic determinants of GCC real exchange rates. The authors find that the money supply, budget balance, government consumption and imports as share of GDP have a similar impact on the real exchange rates across the GCC. Furthermore, the research establishes a long-run equilibrium for the real exchange rates of the GCC and measures the misalignments since 1992. Their findings indicate that despite evidence of convergence over time there was still considerable divergence between the UAE and Oman in 2005. The authors conclude that greater policy coordination and harmonization will be required for MU to be a success; in particular they recommend that a GCC central bank to be established immediately to implement a GCC wide monetary policy and manage GCC liquidity.

Our own econometric analysis (Rutledge 2007) investigates the long-run relationship between each of the GCC economies and the regional economic powerhouse, Saudi Arabia. By adopting a bilateral approach to the analysis it was possible to explore whether the real GDP of each GCC state was trending over the long run with that of Saudi Arabia (see Table 3.6). While the results added to the evidence that the GCC economies have moved together in a long-term relationship since the formation of the GCC, there are some disparities in the long run relationships between the individual GCC economies and Saudi Arabia, possibly indicating the presence of a 'two-speed' GCC. The results indicated that the real GDP of Bahrain and Oman exhibit long-term trending relationships with the Saudi economy forming a 'core' group of countries suitable for MU. However, the UAE and Kuwait did not follow the same long-term growth trend as that of the Saudi economy and can only be considered as 'periphery' in that they are not ideally suited to MU with Saudi Arabia.

The absence of synchronization between the UAE and Saudi Arabia might be rationalized by considering the concerted efforts made by the UAE to integrate into the global economy, liberalizing its economy and opening up to international tourism and FDI at a much greater speed than Saudi Arabia. It has developed an extensive re-export industry and is now reportedly the third largest re-export hub in the world, after Hong Kong and Singapore. It therefore has extensive global trading links which might suggest that the economy is more exposed to global economic trends than regional ones. Our trade analysis at the beginning of this chapter also revealed that the TIR between Saudi Arabia and the UAE was particularly weak.

In the case of Kuwait, having a more independent exchange rate arrangement than the other GCC states for several decades has given it a greater degree of freedom in terms of its monetary policy which may well have allowed it to mitigate regional and domestic shocks to a greater extent than any other GCC economies. Additionally, Kuwait's TIR is generally weak with all its GCC neighbours, including Saudi Arabia.

The importance of being cointegrated with the largest economy in the prospective MU should not be understated and may well have implications for the distribution of costs and benefits of MU to its members. In the absence of strong synchronization between the UAE, the second largest GCC economy, and Saudi Arabia, MU could be costly for either economy and could lead to friction in future monetary policy decision making.

Finally, it must be said that one of the major limitations of such econometric models is that they are retrospective, based on past values of the variables. In the future, it may be the case that if the GCC economies work towards meeting convergence criteria, as did the EMU economies, that with increasing efforts to diversify, deepening trade and capital market integration long-run regional economic synchronization may well grow with time.

To what extent is the GCC an OCA?

While the GCC economies have travelled a considerable way towards meeting the criteria for an OCA, they have not yet done so sufficiently so as to be considered an OCA. This conclusion, however, need not and most likely will not derail the MU project. Not only were the EMU economies not considered to constitute an OCA prior to 1999 but also several criteria are endogenous and the process of preparing for MU – such as establishing a common market – will bring them closer to meeting the economic conditions.

While there is evidence to suggest that intra-GCC trade is more significant than often thought in particular when oil is factored out we contend that this criterion remains insufficiently satisfied so far. However, as the GCC states pursue greater economic diversification it is likely that intra-GCC trade will continue to grow in the coming period.

At present the GCC scores well in terms of labour market mobility, firstly, because there are few legal barriers to national labour mobility and, secondly, because a significant expatriate labour force exists in the region which is highly mobile. However, the expansion of labour nationalization policies across the bloc could seriously erode existing labour market flexibility in the future.

In terms of capital market mobility it is clear that the GCC is moving in the right direction with legislative steps being taken to allow all GCC nationals to invest unhindered in neighbouring markets. Recent evidence reveals that Gulf nationals are keen to cross borders to invest in one another's stock markets, there is significant cross-border cooperation on the issuance of Islamic bonds and intra-GCC FDI has increased substantially since the start of the current oil price boom.

The economies of the GCC states are not well diversified; yet as all of these economies remain *undiversified* in the *same manner* this does not necessarily mean they are unsuitable for MU. However, as diversification occurs it will be important that it takes place *within country* rather than *within region* for this criterion not to be problematic for the future MU. Fortunately, there is preliminary evidence that *within country* diversification is indeed taking place, with increasing competition between GCC states particularly in the downstream oil and gas industry, heavy industry and service sector activities – such as banking and finance and tourism.

With regard to economic synchronization, on the whole the GCC economies appear to be well synchronized over the long run. Yet the majority of econometric studies find evidence of some national anomalies in terms of the degree of synchronization, with Kuwait, Oman and the UAE appearing to be less suitable members for MU. As was the case in Europe, the evidence points to a 'two-speed' GCC where shocks to a 'core' group of countries were closely correlated compared to the shocks facing the 'periphery' countries which were less correlated.

Ultimately, the ability of the GCC states to successfully form an MU will depend more upon the preparations that are made in advance than their structural suitability for MU vis-à-vis the OCA criteria. Yet, we must acknowledge that in the absence of a strong political motivation to integrate the results of the OCA analysis indicating where the costs and benefits of MU lie for the GCC economies could significantly influence the perceived utility of MU for the GCC leaders and, in turn, their level of commitment to the project. In the following chapter therefore we will discuss whether establishing a common currency is a shared political goal of the GCC leaders and whether other prerequisite policies are in place for forming a feasible MU.

4 Policy prerequisites for GCC monetary union

Following the assessment of the GCC's economic suitability for MU against the various OCA criteria, we now turn our attention to MU policy prerequisites and necessary preparations. We consider many of these as essential or at the very least highly desirable in order for a viable MU. Whereas the OCA criteria fall largely into the field of longer term, structural requirements, the factors which we discuss here relate to economic policy variables – the objects of decisions which will have to be made by governments and monetary authorities, ones which in theory can be undertaken within a short timeframe. These policy prerequisites have become apparent primarily as a consequence of the EMU process; therefore, we term these the *European criteria*.

GCC leaders have themselves acknowledged the influence of the European experience in their decision to form an MU. Saudi Arabia's King Abdullah said 'the example of the EU is a model to follow' (Al-Saud 2002). The European Central Bank (ECB) has provided consultation for the GCC Secretariat and the GCC central bank governors provisionally accepted Maastricht-style convergence criteria. However, in light of the very different economic, institutional, cultural, legal and political contexts of the GCC states compared with those of the Eurozone it is questionable as to whether EMU is a viable model for the GCC states to emulate.

While various papers (including Fasano and Staff Team 2003; Sturm and Siegfried 2005; Al-Mansouri and Dziobek 2006) consider the necessary *economic* MU prerequisites for the GCC (quantitative convergence criteria, fiscal rules and institution building), few consider the *political* dimension of these prerequisites in the context of the GCC. This chapter will consider both the economic and political implications of the associated reforms necessary for forming an MU.

This chapter first assesses the GCC's institutional preparations for MU, in particular the setting up of a common market, establishing a GCC central bank and a regional statistical body. It then moves on to examine whether the GCC economies are likely to be able to meet the fiscal and monetary convergence criteria (possibly targets) that they have adopted. It will do this by measuring whether or not the criteria are currently met and against their past performance. This chapter will also consider the extent to which the private sector is being prepared for MU. Finally, it will gauge the extent of political commitment to the process, partly by examining progress to date but also by considering the views of regional experts, interviewed on the subject by this author, including academics, central bankers and government officials.[1]

Institutional preparations

Supranational institutions play an important, perhaps vital, role in strengthening the overall cohesion of a given MU ensuring the smooth functioning of the monetary system and credibility of the single currency. In the case of Europe, supranational institutions played a key role in the integration process. It has been argued that without pan-European institutions, such as the European Commission and the European Monetary Institute (EMI, the precursor to the ECB), EMU would not have become a reality (Leblond 2004). It has been argued that without effective and independent supranational institutions there can be no 'third-party' enforcement of pan-regional agreements (Mattli 1999).

The rentier state characteristics of the GCC has to a certain extent, hindered the development of an effective, independent and strong institutional framework, both at the national and GCC level (Al-Qudsi 2006). The GCC Secretariat is the main supranational institution but it is generally considered as lacking real autonomy and policymaking powers. GCC leaders have been unable so far to agree on the establishment of vital supranational institutions such as a GCC statistical agency and a GCC central bank, while the launch date of the common market has been set back by complications over the completion of the partially implemented customs union.

The customs union and the common market

Article Three of the 2001 Economic Agreement specifically stipulated that a common market should be set up, the final communiqué of the 2006 GCC summit said that it would be in place before the end of 2007. Despite the fact that leaders are taking some steps towards this goal such as enacting legislation to facilitate the free movement of labour and capital the introduction of the common market has been postponed. As this book goes to press a common market has yet to be established, but at the December 2007 GCC summit, it was announced that it would be set up in 2008. Nevertheless, it remains to be seen whether or not a meaningful common market can be completed in this timeframe, as part of the common market it will be important to have a level playing field for businesses across the bloc and this will involve the harmonization of ownership and investment legislation, something as we shall see in Chapter 5 may be difficult to achieve. Nevertheless, most economists consider a common market to be a vital MU prerequisite. Cecchini (1988) argues that a single currency should not be launched without there first being a single market as many of the benefits of MU will not be realized and many of the costs will be amplified.

A functioning common market necessarily includes the completion of the stalled 2003 GCC customs union along with complete factor mobility. Details on establishing the customs union were also included in the 2001 Economic Agreement. The document called for a phased implementation to begin no later than January 2003 and said it would include:

1 A common external customs tariff.
2 Common customs regulations and procedures.
3 Single entry point where customs duties are collected.
4 Elimination of all tariff and non-tariff barriers, while taking into consideration laws of agricultural and veterinarian quarantine, as well as rules regarding prohibited and restricted goods.
5 Goods produced in any Member State shall be accorded the same treatment as national products.

(GCC 2001: Article One)

When the customs union was launched in 2003 it was viewed as a major achievement on the path towards MU. However, although the bloc agreed to harmonize external tariffs at five per cent, the customs union has yet to be fully finalized. This is in large part a result of Bahrain's decision in 2004 to sign a bilateral FTA with the US, which was argued went against the grain of the 2001 Economic Agreement which states that member states would 'negotiate collectively in a manner that serves the negotiating position of the Member States' (GCC 2001: Article Two).

In October 2005 Oman followed Bahrain and became the second GCC state to sign a FTA with the US (Gulf Research Center 2005a). Without Bahrain or Oman revoking their FTAs or the other states negotiating a similar FTA with the US the third and final stage of the customs union – abolishing the customs functions of the intra-GCC border offices – cannot be completed. This is because the other GCC states will still have to levy tariffs on US goods arriving as intra-GCC imports from Bahrain and Oman.

Apparent frustration over the length of time some multilateral FTA negotiations take, for instance those between the GCC and EU which has been on the table for over a decade, may have been a causal factor for such bilateral agreements. In particular, the small economies of Bahrain and Oman, both with minimal oil reserves, may view bilateral FTAs as a necessity both in terms of increasing their non-oil export-led growth strategies and attracting more FDI inflows.

Regardless of the rationale, the issue has set a precedent indicating that the GCC states are willing to flout GCC integration principals and charters if they believe it is in their national interests to do so. The disharmony in trade policy across the GCC states represents a significant stumbling block on their path towards economic integration. In the absence of harmonized trade policies it will be much harder for the GCC states to act as a regional economic bloc in international dealings and negotiations (see Chapter 5 for more discussion of this).

A GCC central bank

As a single currency requires a single monetary policy and therefore a single decision on interest rate movements which must be based upon the economic conditions of the entire regional bloc, it is generally accepted that to have a viable MU there needs to be a supranational central bank. A single central bank means that 'decision-making on a single monetary and exchange rate policy is centralized' (Sturm and Siegfried 2005). Without a strong legal and institutional framework for MU embodied in a single supranational monetary authority individual GCC states may be tempted to give in to their national economic interests and exercise discretion in implementing regional interest rate decisions.

Close cooperation between the supranational central bank and those of the nation states is critical they must cooperate in areas of monetary policy implementation as well as banking and financial regulation and supervision. The formation of a system along the lines of the European System of Central Banks could also be an appropriate mechanism for such cooperation among the national GCC central banks.

Initially the GCC planned to maintain their respective central banks, rather than establish a supranational one, and hold joint meetings to decide on MU policy. Following consultation with the ECB, however, they eventually agreed in principle to create a single GCC central bank. This will involve relinquishing some monetary policy decision-making powers, setting out a single mandate and establishing an organizational structure and legal framework. Yet thus far, most of the debate regarding the creation of a GCC central bank has focused upon the issue of its location (see Chapter 5 for more discussion of this). The EMU experience, however, clearly shows that substantial preparation time will be needed to establish a single central bank. The EMI was set up as a precursor to the ECB and was tasked with carrying out technical research and making monetary preparations four years prior to the electronic launch of the euro and six years before general circulation.

Presently, cooperation between GCC monetary institutions takes place through biannual meetings of the Central Bank Governors' Committee. Additionally, a technical committee meets several times during the year and reports to the aforementioned committee (Rutledge 2007). In 2002 the Supreme Council established a monetary union unit, based at the GCC Secretariat tasked with harmonizing the GCC's money market instruments.[2] According to the GCC Secretariat the legal and institutional requirements for establishing a GCC central bank are also currently under study.

In order to establish an MU along European lines, pan-GCC decisions will have to be taken on the distribution of seigniorage revenues and management of foreign exchange reserves as well as contentious political-economy decisions such as the voting structure of the future monetary policy committee. In the Eurozone, each member state was given equal voting powers regardless of their economic mass. However, Saudi Arabia's position within the GCC is even more significant than that of Germany within EMU; its economic mass and population being equal to or greater than the aggregate sum of all the other five members.

While there may be a compelling economic and political case for allowing Saudi Arabia proportionally more voting power, it may not be particularly appealing to the smaller GCC states. Several regional experts felt that the decision to establish a single supranational monetary authority itself had not been an easy one and that there had been many reservations. According to a Kuwaiti Central Bank official some countries are now having second thoughts regarding the issue of a GCC central bank.

A GCC statistical agency

Common statistical standards and harmonized datasets are particularly important for members of an MU to be able to monitor a nation's adherence to fiscal and monetary rules and for a regional monetary policy committee to be able to make informed decisions based on sound economic data for the region. In EMU various institutions were involved in the collation of comparable regional statistics long in advance of the euro's launch. In 1992, a working group on statistics was set up which liaised with the Statistics Division at the EMI. Nevertheless, and despite of the long lead time, during its early years of operation the ECB still faced policymaking difficulties as a result of missing or lagging data from several countries in the MU (Issing 2004).

The standardization, consistency and disclosure of national statistics in the GCC is far more opaque at present however if compared to the EMU countries in the years leading up to the euro (see Al-Qudsi 2006, Dyer and Yousef 2007). This necessary MU preparation will represent a considerable challenge given the timeframe. There is currently no standardized measure of inflation, base years and the baskets of goods used in producing national CPIs differ from state to state. In the case of the Eurozone states, in order to provide comparable measures of inflation across the region, a new Harmonized Index of Consumer Prices was produced. GCC national datasets themselves are often unreliable, the IMF criticized the current state of statistics in the UAE, commenting that 'the UAE's economic and social statistics continue to suffer from numerous structural weaknesses with respect to data quality, coverage, periodicity, timeliness and inter-sectoral consistency' (IMF 2006a: 19).

In the lead-up to MU all five states will need to individually enact reforms and coordinate institutions to ensure they meet agreed upon standards. Significant lead time to build the institutional capabilities and legal infrastructure for comprehensive data collection will be required (Krueger and Kovarich 2006). It has been recommended that the GCC draw directly on EMU's experience in preparing its statistical base for MU and set up a statistical agency, modelled on Eurostat (Al-Mansouri and Dziobek 2006). 'Gulfstat' would be tasked with developing a common methodology for collecting, standardizing and harmonizing data across the GCC. If the Gulf states do not standardize and share their date in the very near future, not only will it be impossible to assess progress towards convergence and therefore meeting the criteria will continue to be open to interpretation, but it will also make future monetary policy decision making for the bloc unduly complicated.

Fiscal and monetary convergence

At a meeting of GCC central bank governors in September 2005, it was agreed that the council would adopt Maastricht-style convergence criteria. But three months later, in December 2005, Gulf finance ministers failed to approve these targets arguing that they needed more time to consider them (Gulf Research Center 2005b). Although it is hard to find officially published confirmation, according to officials at the GCC Secretariat's Monetary Union Unit, fiscal and monetary convergence targets have now been endorsed by the Economic and Cooperation Committee and by the GCC finance ministers in 2007 (see Table 4.1).

Although in one sense the GCC has already cleared a major hurdle in this regard, all have very similar exchange rate policies and therefore bilateral exchange rates (Kuwait's basket peg has a significant dollar weight), meeting and sticking to government budget deficit and inflation rate criteria will be considerably harder. As Table 4.1 shows, the GCC convergence criteria mirror those of the Maastricht criteria. The objectives of the Maastricht criteria were to achieve important conditions for any prospective MU members – a high degree of price stability, a sustainable government budgetary position and the durability of convergence once MU had been established.

Unlike the EMU convergence criteria which were actually firm and unconditional requirements, the GCC's convergence criteria appear to be more in the nature of targets. In the case of EMU, those states that were not able to meet the criteria were in fact prevented from joining: such was the case with Greece. The question that arises in the case of the GCC convergence criteria therefore is: What will be the incentives for these economies to meet the criteria and how will they be enforced? According to the GCC Monetary Union Unit if a given state cannot meet one or more of the criteria then a meeting will be held to discuss possible measures to deal with this.

As of 2006, only two GCC states – Kuwait and Saudi Arabia – met all of the criteria. Qatar and the UAE are both in breach of the inflation criterion and have been for several years, while Bahrain and the UAE are in breach of the foreign reserves to imports criterion. An empirical analysis of GCC economic data since 1980 illustrates the serious difficulties which these economies will face in trying to meet Maastricht-style criteria which were after all designed for diversified and mature European economies. During that period, for example, Qatar and the UAE would have broken the criteria very frequently and more than any other GCC state (see Table 4.2).

Of the preliminary GCC convergence criteria, only two have been easily achieved in the past: exchange rate stability and interest rate convergence. All six sovereign currencies have exhibited a high degree of exchange rate stability given their historical *de facto* pegs against the dollar (see Figure 4.1). Even the currency of Kuwait – which had a more flexible and discretionary basket peg up until 2003 – showed a high degree of stability, primarily due to a heavy dollar component believed to form the majority share of the basket. Yet in May 2007

Table 4.1 GCC convergence targets and EMU's Maastricht criteria

Criterion	*Maastricht*	*GCC*
1 Exchange rates	Exchange rate fluctuation within the normal margins for two years without any devaluation against any other member states currency	Long-term stability of GCC exchange rates has meant that this criterion has not been considered[a]
2 Foreign reserves	No such criterion	Foreign reserves to cover four months of imports
3 Interest rates	Long-term interest rates must not exceed more than 2% of that of the three best performing countries (in terms of price stability)	As Maastricht, but for short-term interests (three months)
4 Inflation rates	Inflation rates must not exceed more than 1.5% of the average of the three best performing countries	As Maastricht
5 Fiscal deficits	Government deficits must not exceed 3% of GDP[b]	Budget deficit must not exceed 3% of GDP when oil prices are $25/b or above[c]
6 Fiscal debt	Government debt must not exceed 60% of GDP	Government debt must not exceed 60% of GDP for the general government and 70% of GDP for the central government

Source: Rutledge 2008a.

Notes

a This may now need to be reconsidered following Kuwait's reversion to a basket peg in May 2007 and the announcement by GCC central bank governors in September 2007 that each state may pursue individual exchange rate policies in order to tackle rising inflation.

b This rule however, was not binding under certain economic circumstances see Eichengreen and Wyplosz (1998).

c This is based on OPEC basket price. If prices fall below $25/b, the maximum deficit is based on the formula: $\text{Deficit}(t) = 3 + 3[(25 - \text{Price}(t-1))/25]$.

Table 4.2 Number of historical convergence criteria breaches, 1980–2006

Criterion	*Bahrain*	*Kuwait*	*Oman*	*Qatar*	*KSA*	*UAE*
Foreign reserves	8	1	9	8	2	10
Interest rate	0	3	0	0	0	0
Inflation rate	6	15	3	21	2	23
Fiscal deficit	5	12	18	13	16	20
Fiscal debt[a]	0	0	0	0	8	0
Total breaches[b]	19	31	30	42	28	53

Source: Rutledge 2008a.

Notes

a Fiscal debt data starts from 1997.

b Each breach represents one criterion being broken in one year, therefore if two criteria were broken in every year since 1980 the country would have 54 breaches in total.

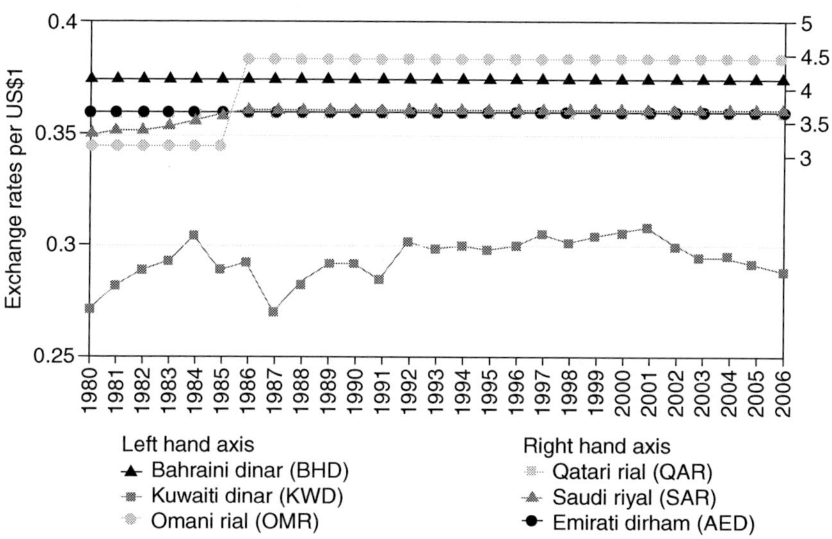

Figure 4.1 GCC nominal exchange rates against the US$, 1980–2006 (source: IMF (2007d)).

the Kuwait Central Bank officially reverted back to a basket peg, allowing a moderate revaluation of the dinar against the falling dollar at the same time.

Despite having reneged on a key preparation towards MU, given the heavy dollar weighting in Kuwait's currency basket the dinar is likely to continue to be relatively stable against the other GCC currencies. Given the region's preference for fixed exchange rates the GCC added a non-Maastricht criteria: that of holding reserves equal to cover four months of imports. The sustainability of the GCC pegs against the dollar has been supported by the large levels of international reserves which the GCC states hold, which have deterred speculative activity against their currencies.

An analysis of GCC foreign reserve cover to imports indicates that only Saudi Arabia and Kuwait have held sufficiently large reserves to achieve the criterion of four months reserve cover to imports for prolonged periods without breaching it. Both the UAE and Bahrain breached this criterion as recently as 2006, when their reserves fell to 3.4 and 2.6 months of import cover respectively (see Figure 4.2). For Bahrain it was the third consecutive year of not meeting the criterion, its reserve cover has fallen annually since 2001.

Historically the GCC states have been able to meet the interest rate criterion with little difficulty. There have however, been a few occasions in the past when Kuwait would have broken the interest rate convergence rule, such as during the 1991 Gulf war when interest rates were raised in an attempt to prevent capital flight (see Figure 4.3). Kuwait has however had more interest rate flexibility than the other GCC states as it has been pegged to a basket of currencies.

GCC interest rates have shown a considerable degree of convergence over the period of study (in EMU this criterion was for long-term interest rate convergence, in the GCC it is for short-term interest rate convergence), because the region's interest rates having moved in line with US rates and concomitantly with each other. Since reaching a peak in 1992 the GCC interest rate spread has narrowed and was just less than one per cent in 2006 (see Figure 4.4).

The ability of the GCC states to meet the inflation convergence criterion will be considerably harder. Since 1980 there has not been a single year in which all five states would have met the criterion, which stipulates that inflation levels must not exceed 1.5 per cent of the average of the three best performing members (see Figure 4.5). The UAE, followed by Qatar and Kuwait have breached the rule most frequently, in fact, the last time the UAE would have been able to meet the target was in 1990.

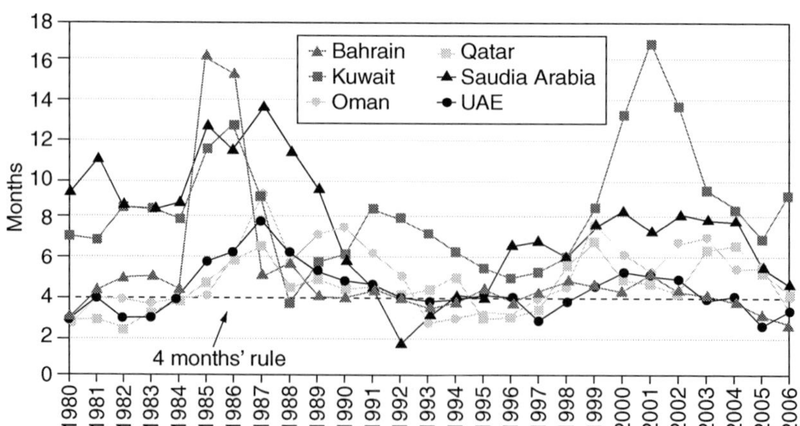

Figure 4.2 Reserve cover to months of imports, 1980–2006 (sources: AMF (2006 and previous issues); IMF (2007b, 2007c); SAMA (2007)).

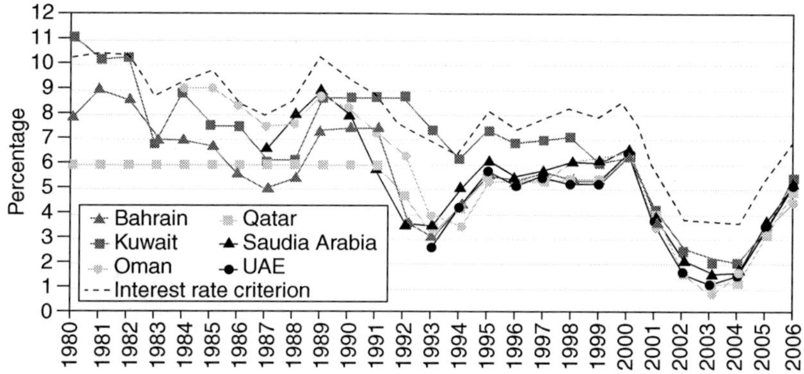

Figure 4.3 GCC short-term interest rates, 1980–2006 (sources: Author's calculations of interest rate criterion based on data from and SAMA (2007); IMF (2007d).

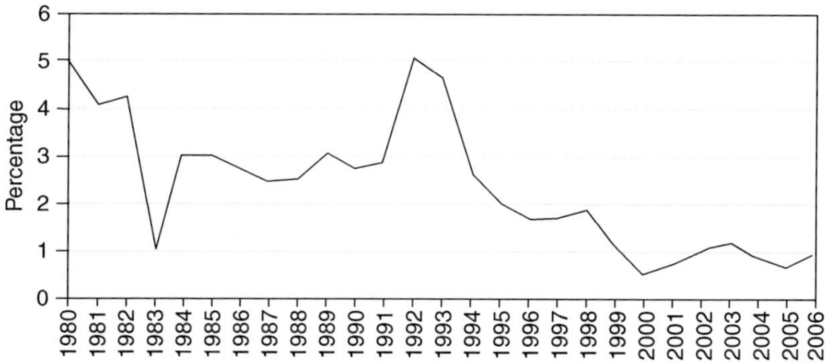

Figure 4.4 GCC interest rate spread, 1980–2006 (sources: SAMA (2007); IMF (2007d).

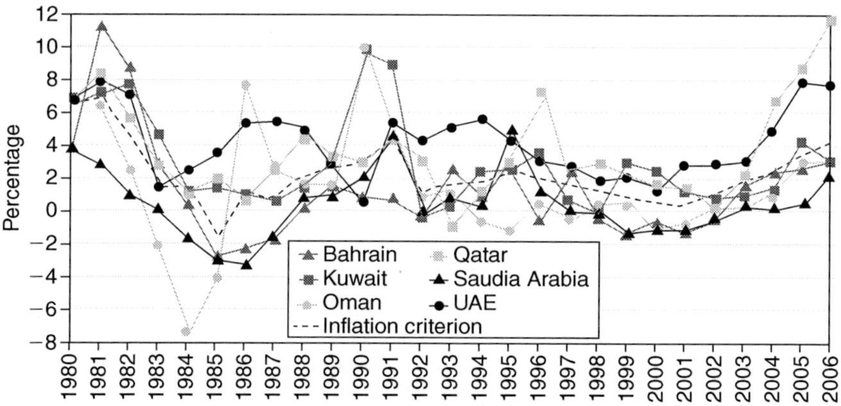

Figure 4.5 GCC inflation rates, 1980–2006 (source: Author's calculations for inflation criterion, based on data from IMF (2007a).

For example, average inflation in the UAE between 1980 and 2006 was 3.9 per cent but in Saudi Arabia it was only 0.51 per cent. It seems that the GCC can be segmented into two inflationary sub-regions: a low inflation region: Bahrain, Oman and Saudi Arabia and a high inflation region: Kuwait, Qatar and the UAE. Inflation divergence has once again widened during the current oil price boom reaching almost ten per cent in 2006 (see Figure 4.6).

Econometric evidence suggests that there are in fact persistent deviations from purchasing power parity across the GCC economies (Hassanain 2004), some of the underlying reasons for price level deviation were discussed in chapter two. Even in light of Frankel and Rose's (1997) proposition that convergence may be endogenous to the process of forming MU, it is difficult to conceive how inflation rate divergence of this magnitude could be tolerated in advance of forming MU. Indeed, as we shall discuss in Chapter 5, there is increasing divergence among GCC policymakers as to how best to deal with widening inflation differentials.

Qatar's Central Bank has suggested that core inflation be used as the measure of inflation convergence, stripping out in particular the cost of rent and housing. At the time of writing the GCC Monetary Union Unit was seriously investigating this possibility. Core inflation data is not made publicly available by any of these states at present but the GCC Monetary Union Unit is confident that using this measure of inflation will remove the difficulty in meeting this particular criterion.

Of course, inflation differentials were also a cause for concern in the run-up to the launch of the euro. As the launch date approached member states adjusted their fiscal and monetary policies in order to meet the rules and rates began to converge (Egert *et al.* 2004). The inflation rate spread between the Eurozone countries decreased dramatically from as much as to 20 per cent in the beginning of the 1990s to around only one per cent by mid-1999. However, unlike the Eurozone, the GCC will not be able to use monetary policy tools (i.e. raising or lowering interest rates) to achieve price convergence in the lead-up to MU, so

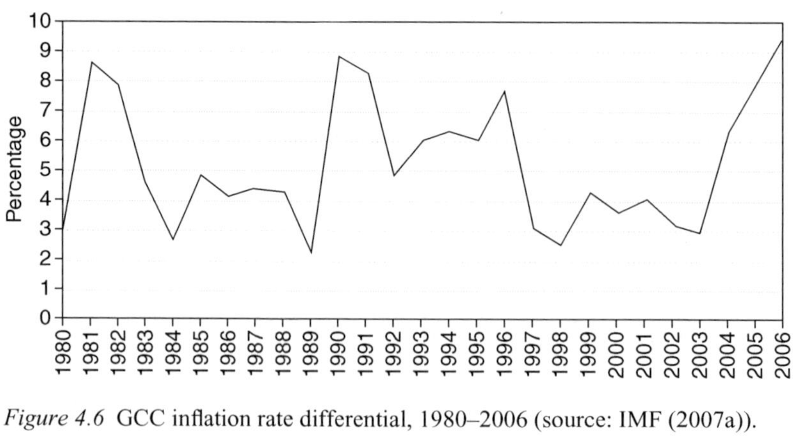

Figure 4.6 GCC inflation rate differential, 1980–2006 (source: IMF (2007a)).

the onus will be on fiscal restraint. Yet, enacting tighter fiscal discipline now would jeopardize some of the government-led economic diversification and development plans currently in full swing.

Turning to fiscal rules, after several years of high oil prices all five prospective MU members are currently able to meet the fiscal criteria, however, in the past these rules would have been repeatedly breached. The fiscal rules in the Maastricht Treaty, later enshrined in the Stability and Growth Pact (SGP) were designed to prevent undisciplined spenders 'free-riding' on the credibility of other more fiscally prudent members (Eichengreen and Wyplosz 1998). Measures and safeguards to restrict the level of government budget deficits, and debt, are considered critical to the sustainability of an MU. According to the GCC Monetary Union Unit the fiscal deficit rule has been marginally adjusted to reflect the region's economic characteristics. Adjustments will only occur during years of low oil prices whereby if the OPEC basket price falls below $25/b, the maximum deficit in the present year is based on the formula where as the oil price in the previous year converges to zero the deficit will be increased to a maximum of six per cent. Despite this, looking back at historical data this GCC-modified criterion would still have been broken on numerous occasions; in the 1990s when the oil price was often below $25/b, deficits higher than ten per cent of GDP were not uncommon in several GCC states (see Figure 4.7).

GCC fiscal policy management continues to be problematic: the income base of regional governments is very narrow depending largely on income derived from oil and gas revenues. In 2005, almost four-fifths of GCC government revenues were derived from oil and gas, little changed from a decade earlier. Repeated budget deficit offenders have been the largest GCC economies – Saudi

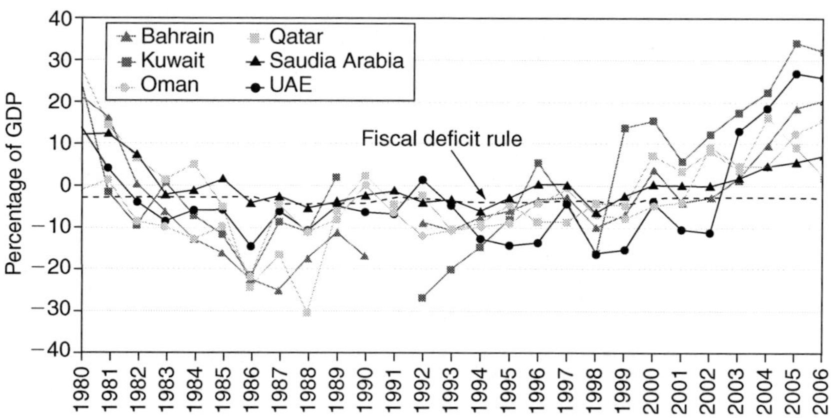

Figure 4.7 GCC government deficits to GDP ratios, 1980–2006 (sources: Author's calculations based on data from Al-Uwaisheg (2003); IMF (2007c) data).

Note: Official data for Kuwait is missing for years 1990–1991 and for Saudi Arabia for 1991 most likely as a consequence of the 1991 Gulf war.

Arabia and the UAE. Figures for the UAE's government budget have to be interpreted with caution as the budget at the federal level does not take into account income returns on investments abroad which would have often offset any deficit. Presumably, this is why, after years of deficits, the UAE has not needed to issue much public debt.

Historically, GCC fiscal policies have been highly procyclical as government spending has been correlated with oil prices. During times of low oil prices fiscal expenditure has been cut back rather than expanded as one might expect if an active fiscal policy were being pursued (Fasano and Wang 2002). Such procyclical fiscal policies were identified in many Eurozone countries prior to MU and the fiscal prudence rules contained in the SGP were designed in order to limit this practice. Yet due to increased spending during times of high oil prices many states have not been able to build up sufficient surpluses to cover the deficits incurred during periods of prolonged low oil prices.

As part of their MU preparation process, and even at this late stage, the GCC may need to reconsider their fiscal criteria and make them more attuned with the stage of economic development they are currently at and to factor in the inherent volatility of oil, rather than adopting EMU rules which themselves have been questioned. Some of the diversified economies of the Eurozone faced great difficulty in meeting the deficit to GDP ratio and several have broken the criterion since 1999. As a consequence, in 2005, the SGP was reformed allowing for a series of economic exceptions to the criterion and making the fiscal criteria somewhat less rigid.

Turning to the debt to GDP criteria, the GCC criterion is slightly differentiated from that of EMU in that it distinguishes between general government and central government debt. While general government debt must not exceed 60 per cent of GDP the limit for central government debt is 70 per cent of GDP. Central government refers to the federal government whereas the general government includes all levels of government, including public institutions and government enterprises. However, in order to measure the two levels of government debt careful examination of the classification of government and government-related institutions will be required.

At present there is no data available which distinguishes between the two and it is questionable whether such data is made available to the GCC Secretariat considering that their data tends to be collated from published national data sources. Nevertheless, according to secretariat statistics on public sector debt, dating back to 1997, most GCC states have been within the lower limit of the 60 per cent debt to GDP ratio in the past, with the notable exception of Saudi Arabia (see Figure 4.8). Nevertheless, all of the GCC states currently meet this criterion.

Preparing the private sector

A key preparation for MU will be preparing the region's private sector for the transition to the new monetary system. The transition to MU is likely to produce

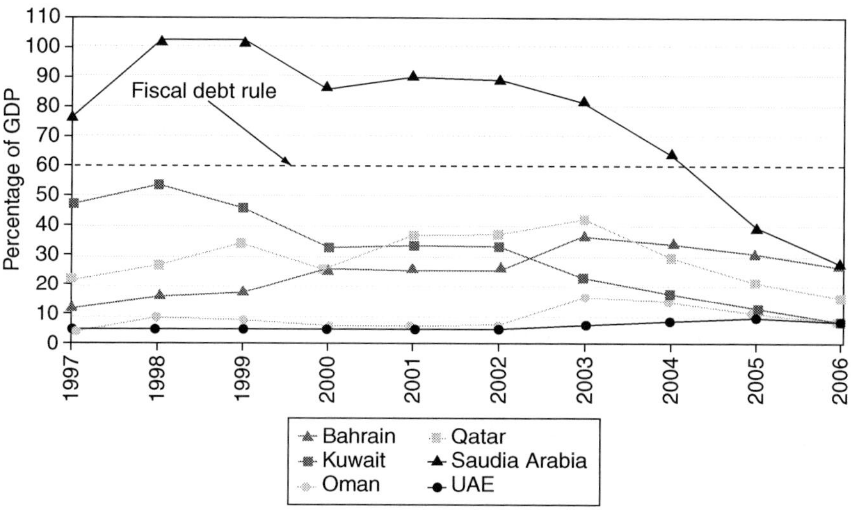

Figure 4.8 GCC debt to GDP ratios, 1997–2006 (sources: Author's calculations based on data from Al-Uwaisheg (2003); IMF (2007c) data).

important indirect effects which materialize through adjustments in the behaviour of economic agents to the change in economic system (Commission of the European Communities 1990). Private sector expectations about price stability and monetary credibility – which are influenced by the provision of information – are crucial in determining future investment decisions and consequently economic growth. GCC policymakers will need to inform, educate and prepare businesses in order to ensure economic confidence and smooth the transition to the single currency.

The findings of the GCC business survey – which, in part, sought to ascertain their preparedness for and attitudes towards MU – underlined the fact that GCC businesses were not at all prepared for MU and that this was a concern for them in light of the scheduled deadline. Of the survey respondents not a single business said they were currently making preparations for the single currency although just over a quarter of respondents said that they would do so closer to 2010.

At the time of the survey there was still ample time for the region's governments and the GCC Secretariat to prepare businesses (with five years until the launch date), but since the survey little, if any, specific information has been disseminated to businesses with regard to preparing for MU. Considering the lack of policy and institutional preparations for MU already discussed in this chapter it is hardly surprising that the GCC governments have yet to begin preparing the private sector for the launch of the single currency. Yet in 2005 the majority of business respondents – 59 per cent – felt that governments should be providing information with regard to preparing for MU. Slightly more than one-third of business respondents, 35 per cent, felt that governments should provide information and assistance closer to 2010 (Rutledge 2008b). This finding indicates the private sector's desire for greater transparency regarding the MU project.

In the case of EMU, concerted efforts to inform the European business community and prepare them for the launch of the single currency took place at least three years prior to the introduction of the euro. Earlier still, between 1995 and 1998, communication campaigns were launched in order to inform businesses of the timetable for switching to the euro. Dual pricing was also widespread in all member states several years before the introduction of the euro where labels showed the price in both the national currency and the euro.

The survey results also illustrate that business uncertainty about the transition to the new monetary system may be costly for the private sector. The experience of EMU shows that businesses can expect to incur some initial transitional costs from the launch of a single currency. Businesses will be required to adapt their information technology, accounting, marketing, pricing and payroll systems in advance of the launch of the single currency and they must be made aware that this will only be a one-off cost if they are to see the process in a favourable light.

However, only 12 per cent of business respondents thought that the MU would initially increase their costs, the majority of business respondents – 52 per cent – were unsure as to whether it would and 37 per cent thought it would not increase their costs (Rutledge 2008b). More than any other size of company it was SMEs that felt the MU would temporarily increase their costs, with 47 per cent believing so. Unlike larger companies, SMEs may find it harder to absorb any increase in their costs resulting from the MU and therefore are more likely to be considering this factor. As several GCC states are developing and enacting policies to foster the growth of SMEs it would be wise for them to provide assistance to these businesses on preparing for MU as soon as possible.

GCC businesses will need to be driven to make timely preparations well in advance of the launch date for a single currency and policymakers will have to take concerted action to inform, educate and assist businesses in this regard. In Europe, despite campaigns to inform and prepare the private sector from early on by 1998 the business community was still not fully prepared for the monetary transition, in particular SMEs were falling behind (KPMG, 1998). However, until the GCC business community is convinced that MU will actually take place at a future date they are unlikely to be willing to invest time and money in adjusting their systems for a switch to a single currency. It is clear therefore that until GCC governments begin to make unambiguous progress in preparing for MU, businesses will be reluctant to act.

Political commitment and motivation

Existing research suggests that many of the traditional economic OCA criteria may be endogenous: in that the political decision and clear commitment to establishing an MU *itself* facilitates the economic adjustments required for the satisfaction of the OCA criteria (Frankel and Rose 1996). In this respect it could be said that political commitment to MU itself becomes a major policy prerequisite.

However, establishing the level of political commitment to GCC MU is not a straightforward task, due to the opaque nature of decision making at the highest level. In addition to the evidence provided by the pace of progress to date, we can also examine the possible motivations behind the GCC leaders' decision to establish MU. As we shall argue, there may be an important relationship between the type of motivation which drives the decision making process for MU, on the one hand and, on the other, the intensity of the political commitment to reaching that objective.

So far in this chapter we have established that the GCC states have yet to enact many key prerequisites that are generally considered essential steps towards establishing a viable MU. According to Balassa's (1961) five stages of increasing degrees of regional integration (a free trade area, a customs union, a common market, an economic union (including some harmonization of economic policies) and finally complete economic integration), EMU is arguably somewhere between stages four and five, whereas the GCC states presently appear to be stuck at stage two. The lack of tangible progress in terms of regional economic integration since 1981 certainly seems to suggest only a lukewarm political commitment to the project.

Evidence from regional interviews reveals a commonly held perception among experts that the political commitment of the region's leaders to see the process through is lacking. The largest proportion of experts interviewed believed that the 2010 launch date for MU would not be achieved and that it would be delayed (Rutledge 2007). Approximately 38 per cent did not expect the MU to be established as scheduled, while 28 per cent said they 'hoped so' or 'maybe' leaving only 26 per cent who said they thought it would be established on schedule (see Figure 4.9). Of those experts that felt the MU would not be

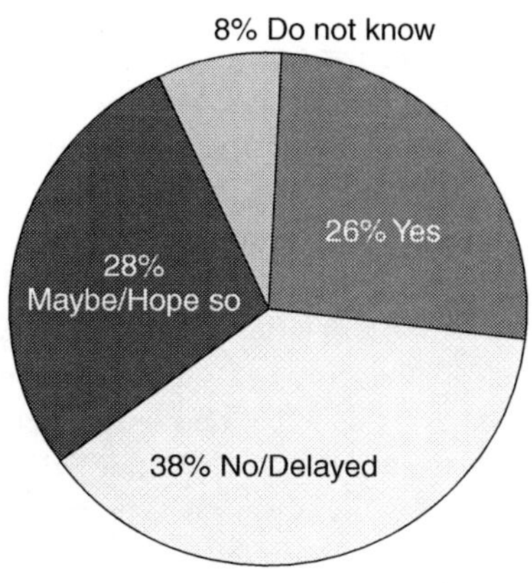

Figure 4.9 Expert interviewees: 'Will GCC MU be on schedule?' (source: Rutledge (2007)).

established by 2010 most said that they thought it would be delayed by a period of between two to five years. However, a few government officials felt inclined to say that it might not be established in the foreseeable future.

In the case of Europe, it is clear that both the formation of a common market and the establishment of MU were driven more by a political motive rather than being based on economic merits alone (Feldstein 1997; Willett 2000). Despite some major economic disparities between its members, EMU succeeded because of the perceived political advantages of greater unity. The evidence from EMU suggests that the motivation behind establishing MU is a major factor determining political commitment.

EMU has been seen by some observers as a means to achieving lasting peace through greater political cohesion in Europe and indeed such rationale was initially stated by the architects of EMU. Willett (2000) argues that the process of economic integration in Europe which culminated in a single currency secured primary national security and foreign policy goals for its main architects. The EMU experience indicates that the stronger the role of political, as opposed to economic, considerations in motivating the participants of a potential MU, the stronger will be the political commitment to the process of implementing it.

Admittedly the evidence for this proposition is scant since there have been so few MUs formed from scratch, but, as we have said, the experience of EMU certainly supports it and furthermore the experience of other MUs does not contradict it. The French franc zones, which have existed for over half a century, are a legacy of the monetary institutions that were in place during French colonial rule, therefore membership of the union was imposed on the region and not necessarily elected for by the respective member governments. The ECCU also evolved from a colonial past and colonial institutions such as the British Caribbean Currency Board.

It may be revealing therefore that the largest proportion of GCC expert interviewees – 34 per cent – felt that the motivation behind establishing GCC MU was based on economic considerations, followed by 25 per cent who thought the motivation was political and 22 per cent who believed that 'emulating the success of the EMU' was the main source of motivation (see Figure 4.10).

Indeed, the unsteady rate of progress towards MU illustrates the primary role of economic considerations, with commitment to achieving integration inversely related to the price of oil. Although the signing of the 1981 Economic Agreement marked the beginning of the bloc's economic integration aspirations, it was not until the 2001 summit, after a decade of depressed oil prices, poor growth performance and rising national unemployment that the GCC once again saw the utility of economic integration as a means of diversifying away from an overdependence on oil. Since the start of the current oil price boom the pace of progress has undoubtedly faltered it may be that the huge oil revenue windfalls which have accrued to the GCC states and the resulting economic upswing since 2002 has simply reduced the economic imperative to integrate.

Furthermore, despite minor border disputes, none of which has ever led to armed conflict, the GCC states face no major political imperative to pursue eco-

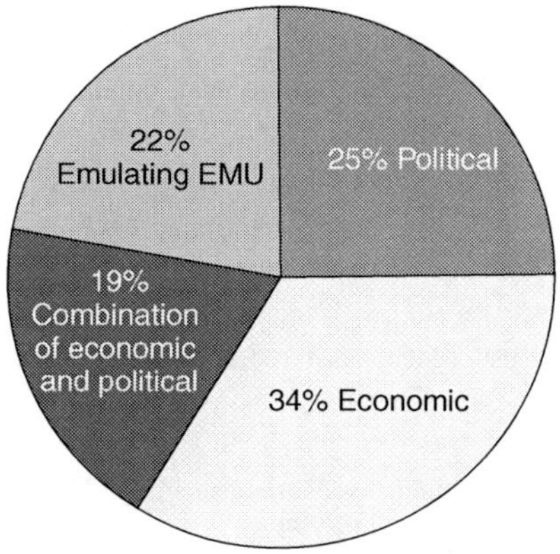

Figure 4.10 Expert interviewees: 'What is the motivation for GCC MU?' (source: Rutledge (2007)).

nomic integration for security reasons alone. Indeed, there is already some, albeit meagre, cooperation on regional security issues, with the establishment of a regional 'rapid reaction force'. Nevertheless regional security concerns over Iran's domineering role in the region were considered to be the major impetus behind the formation of the GCC itself (Aarts 1999). Therefore the current political turbulence in the Gulf (the sectarian power struggle in Iraq and Iran's continuing standoff with the US) may once again bring the GCC countries to a greater awareness of the overall gains that can be obtained from much greater economic and political integration, of which the formation of successful MU is but one part, albeit a very important one.

Are the European criteria being addressed?

It would appear in some ways that the GCC states fair better in terms of their suitability for MU vis-à-vis OCA criteria than they do in terms of meeting the European criteria prior to 2010. Outstanding challenges include finalizing the customs union establishing a common market, deciding upon the mandate and location of a single central bank, a better dissemination and standardization of national economic data and either working towards meeting the current GCC convergence criteria or revising them to better suit the economic fundamentals of the region.

Despite intending to emulate the EMU blueprint and indeed following much direct consultations with the ECB, it is clear that much remains to be done. One important lesson the Eurozone can and should provide the GCC with is that the creation of strong supranational institutions with adequate levels of autonomy and decision-making powers are essential, for anything but the loosest form of MU. The euro's success has in large part been attributed to the existence of effective supranational institutions which supported the setting up of the common market and single currency and acted as a 'third-party' enforcer for implementing agreements.

While we have argued with regard to some convergence criteria that the GCC may find it more appropriate to develop ones specific to their economic characteristics, as they are at a different stage of economic development than are their European counterparts, EMU remains the best general model to follow. This is because it is the only MU in recent times to have been designed and entered into voluntarily by its constituent members. Institutions such as the ECB and Eurostat, in our view, are the most important items the GCC should seek to *emulate*, while the convergence criteria should be used as a guideline, not a *blueprint*.

Finally, the EMU experience illustrates, that above all else, there needs to be a strong political desire and/or motive to enter into MU. While in the past regional leaders seem to have been motivated by the economic merits of the project many that by any assumed political considerations, the current oil price boom has undoubtedly reduced the imperative to push ahead with economic integration plans at this point in time. Thus the political costs and benefits – real or imagined – may now have a greater bearing on whether or not the GCC MU project is launched on schedule or not. In the following chapters, we cover the likely political costs and benefits resulting from the project in conjunction with the economic and wider geopolitical ones.

5 Potential costs of GCC monetary union

That there are costs as well as benefits involved in the establishment of a GCC MU should now have begun to become clear from the analysis in the previous chapters. Whether these costs become actual obstacles to its establishment depends on two crucial factors. First, whether the collective gains to the GCC states are perceived as outweighing those costs (the subject of our next chapter) and, second, whether the costs are shared collectively and uniformly throughout the region: because if the latter were indeed the case, it is much less likely that the project would go ahead. Fortunately, as this chapter will clarify, this is not the case; different GCC states encounter different costs in joining an MU and in such a situation, the door is left open for a process of discussion, bargaining and, hopefully, compromise, in which wise counsel may come to predominate over narrow nationalistic instincts and the greater good prevail over sectional interests.

However, rather than adopt a country-by-country approach to the costs of MU, it will be more convenient to discuss the main categories of cost in their generality while at the same time indicating which particular GCC states are most likely to incur which particular costs. Four main categories of cost can be identified. First, those involved in relinquishing monetary policy independence; second, those arising from the harmonization of differing existing national economic strategies (in the fields of trade, investment and labour policy); third, the potential costs that may arise from the process of implementing Maastricht-style fiscal convergence criteria; and, fourth, a range of issues which one might describe as 'political costs': primarily fears (real or imaginary) of losing sovereign powers or that one or another state within the GCC may gain an unacceptable level of dominance in the new economic bloc and whose internal social, economic and political outlook may threaten those of other GCC states – and here the inevitable focus is upon the Kingdom of Saudi Arabia.

Into this category of political costs also falls the issue of 'who gains and who loses'. Some of the necessary reforms required for MU to take place will be considered as either *beneficial* or *costly* depending upon which sector of society is consulted. For example, in some Gulf states financial data relating to incomes and expenditures is opaque and will need to be reformed. While this would be considered as a *benefit* by investors both domestic and foreign, it might also be viewed as a *cost* by those who benefit from such an opaque state of affairs – some ruling elites and those closely attached to them.

Although this chapter will illustrate that the potential costs of a GCC MU may, in fact, be greater and more varied than previous studies have indicated; it is our view that most are manageable and their magnitude will very much depend on the level of political commitment to the process and degree of preparations undertaken in advance of the final move to MU. If the prerequisite political will is in place the costs are likely to be perceived as being outweighed by the benefits. The latter are set out in Chapter 6 while it is left to Chapter 7 to provide a preliminary cost/benefit balance sheet.

Finally, we note that the creation of an MU will inevitably involve some short-term transitional costs. These include potential inflationary pressures resulting from the rounding up of prices during the conversion of five sovereign currencies to the single Gulf dinar and the one-off costs to businesses from adjusting their accounting, vending and payments systems for the single currency. However, due to the essentially short-term nature of these, we do not give coverage to them here and instead focus on the longer term and more fundamental cost elements.

Relinquishing independent monetary policy

The loss of sovereign control over monetary policy is conventionally considered to be the main cost resulting from MU. Hitherto, various studies concluded that there will be little cost to the GCC states in this regard because they have had bilateral exchange rate stability and similar monetary policies for several decades (see for example Jadresic 2002; Fasano and Staff Team 2003). Indeed, in 2003 all GCC states officially pegged their respective currencies to the dollar as an interim step towards locking in bilateral exchange rates in advance of 2010.

However, since then, economic circumstances have changed and the dollar peg has become an issue of growing controversy. The increasingly weak dollar exacerbated by US interest rate cuts has combined with rising domestic inflation rates to prompt some GCC leaders to question the utility of continuing to peg to the US dollar. By 2007, the traditionally conservative GCC central bankers were openly debating its utility. Kuwait's decision to abandon the collective peg in May 2007 illustrates that one of the convergence areas where the GCC were once considered to be performing remarkably well (Sturm and Siegfried 2005) now represents a potential stumbling block. Kuwait has made it clear that if MU means a dollar peg, then this is one step towards MU it is not willing to take (which is not to say that Kuwait is challenging the principle of MU per se).

However, Kuwait's decision certainly injected a note of acrimony into what was previously a rather muted public debate on MU. Highlighting diverging interests on this issue, Omani Central Bank governor, Hamood Al-Zadjali, announced that in his view the Kuwaiti monetary policy was clearly at odds with that of Oman's stating that 'no developing country aiming at diversification and export promotion, can afford a policy of exchange rate appreciation' (Kumar 2006). Rather than being concerned about the inflationary costs of European imports, Al-Zadjali saw nominal depreciation as advantageous for Oman's diversification strategy. This preference for a relatively weak currency may, as we have previously mentioned, partially explains Oman's decision to withdraw from the MU project altogether in December 2006.

In December 2007 Bahrain's Central Bank governor, Rasheed Al-Maraj, dismissed speculation that a revaluation of the Bahraini dinar would occur in 2008 as 'similar to the rumor that Elvis was seen in Bahrain' (Husain 2007). Although to a lesser extent than Bahrain and Oman, Saudi Arabia may also see advantages in a weaker currency as it would help keep its petrochemical exports competitively priced. But its reluctance to move away from the dollar peg may also have something to do with not wanting to displease the US administration (see Chapter 8 for more on this).

Qatar and the UAE, with large hydrocarbon endowments and a preference for European goods, are likely to see a monetary policy similar to that of Kuwait's basket peg as optimal for their own economies. The UAE central bank governor, Sultan Al-Suwaidi, has often suggested that a more flexible exchange rate policy would be preferable and, stated in November 2007, that 'the depreciation of the dollar had placed the UAE at a "crossroads" over the dirham's dollar peg' (Augustine 2007b). We now consider Qatar to be at a similar crossroads.

Based on a Philips curve analysis, De Grauwe (1975) argued that a convergence of governments' preferences regarding the trade-off between inflation and unemployment was a crucial prerequisite for MU. In the Arabian Peninsula, however, national unemployment is more a consequence of structural factors rather than cyclical ones (see *Labour market mobility* in Chapter 4). Nevertheless the differing preferences for growth and inflation among the GCC states will ideally need to converge in the coming years for a single monetary policy to be considered appropriate.

Despite the UAE having the region's highest inflation rates in 2007 the Dubai government, announced plans to achieve compound annual growth of 11 per cent leading to a trebling of its economy by 2015 (Kerr 2007b). Saudi Arabia, contrariwise, has appeared willing to use fiscal policy as a means of keep inflation rates under control. In May 2007 Saudi Finance Minister, Ibrahim Al-Assaf, announced that the Kingdom would cut current expenditure if necessary to reduce inflation: 'Price stability is a challenge and we are working to make sure the size of spending does not affect economic development' (Reuters 2007).

Despite facing common oil price shocks, their responses have clearly not been uniform (see Chapter 3). This is not due solely to the increasingly heterogeneous development and growth strategies among the different GCC states (see next section) but also because of the clear divergence of their inflation rates (see Figure 5.1). A statistical examination of GCC inflation rates shows that in many cases they are not highly correlated (Laabas and Limam 2002) indeed in some instances there appears to be negative correlation between the inflation rates of Saudi Arabia and the UAE and between those of Kuwait and Saudi Arabia while

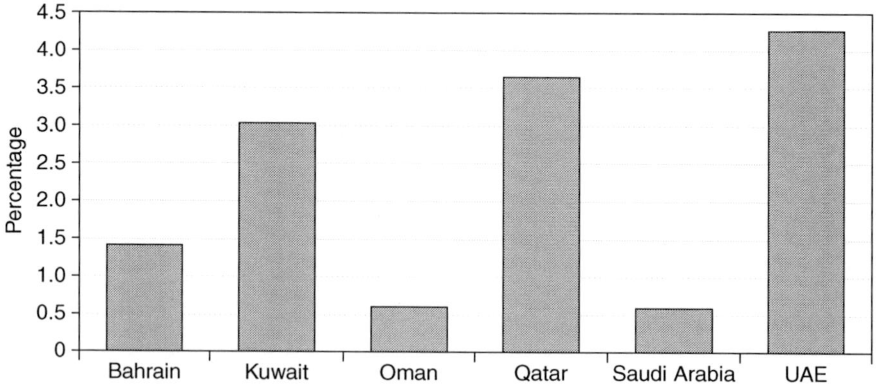

Figure 5.1 GCC average inflation rates, 1980–2006 (source: Author's calculations based on data from IMF(2007a)).

Table 5.1 GCC CPI correlation analysis, 1996–2006

	Bahrain	*Kuwait*	*Oman*	*Qatar*	*KSA*	*UAE*
Bahrain	1					
Kuwait	0.657829	1				
Oman	0.826439	0.467199	1			
Qatar	0.825006	0.952302	0.695032	1		
KSA	0.445053	–0.23943	0.675127	0.056417	1	
UAE	0.782279	0.975122	0.60502	0.99071	–0.03373	1

Source: Calculated by author using data from IMF (2007a).

the correlation between Qatar and Saudi Arabia is also very low at close to zero (see Table 5.1).

Without tackling the root causes in advance of MU, inflation may become more entrenched in the high inflation sub-group (Kuwait, Qatar and the UAE), at a cost to their future competitive position within the bloc and indeed their macroeconomic stability. This would be all the more likely if the post-MU joint monetary policy had a bias towards the dominant (relatively lower inflation) Saudi economy. The ramifications may be significant, according to Nitsch: 'a large inflation differential between currency union members is consistently associated with a high likelihood of a currency union dissolution' (Nitsch 2005: 342).

Taken together, the developments described above indicate that from a dynamic perspective, the potential loss of sovereign control over monetary and exchange rate policy could now be perceived by GCC leaders as a more significant cost than had been previously considered.

Harmonizing differing national economic strategies

According to Balassa (1961) the harmonization of macroeconomic policies and strategic policy preferences is an important prerequisite for deeper economic integration. In our view, it is especially necessary for prospective members of an MU. Diverging economic policies will most likely lead to divergence in the macroeconomic performance of the group of countries contemplating MU and consequently in the medium to longer term the 'one size fits all' monetary policy implicit in MU could be increasingly perceived as economically inappropriate.

Indeed, there is already evidence that some Gulf states are beginning to consider the costs of re-aligning individual country economic strategies in a manner which makes their economic performance consistent with the objective of MU as excessive. There are a wide range of policy issues (including some more relevant at the micro-level) which could be considered in this context. One particularly important policy variable – fiscal policy – we leave to the next section of this chapter, given its particular significance. For now we briefly review three policy areas – external trade policy, investment and employment – where divergent strategies have already opened up and the countries in question may have to re-assess the benefits they might hope to gain from MU against the costs of re-aligning those policy choices in a manner more consistent with MU.

External trade policy

External trade policy is one such area where different approaches have already begun to undermine the progress towards integration and where the costs of reversing this process could prove particularly intractable. The US, unlike the EU, has sought to negotiate FTAs with each of the GCC states individually although, thus far, only Bahrain in 2004 and Oman in 2005 have broken ranks and agreed FTAs. Nevertheless, by giving US goods and services free access to these economies the FTAs have created complications for the bloc as a whole: because if Bahraini or Omani companies were to re-export these to their neighbours they would have an 'unfair advantage' as other GCC states impose nominal tariffs on US goods. Consequently, the four other GCC states are likely to impose tariffs on Bahraini and Omani re-exports of US goods contravening the single point of entry customs duties collection rule in Article One detailing the customs union in the 2001 Economic Agreement (see Chapter 4). Saudi Arabia unusually made public its displeasure at such bilateral FTAs labelling Bahrain's move as a 'clear violation of the GCC's economic accords and decisions' and that it would 'impede the progressive steps needed to achieve full GCC economic integration' (*Arab News* 2004a).

It is probably true that the signing of the Bahraini and Omani FTAs, were the consequence of the final stage of the GCC customs union planned for the end of 2006 being put on hold for several years. Furthermore, it indicates that some states are willing to jeopardize the process of regional economic integration should they consider it to be in their immediate commercial and economic interests to do so. The problem that has now been created, however, is that persuading these two countries to revoke or renegotiate their FTAs may be difficult because of the costs involved, neither are larger GCC states likely to want to accept the same FTAs as those negotiated by Bahrain and Oman. Not only will those economic sectors within Bahrain and Oman which have benefited from the agreements be required to abandon the economic advantages they have gained but there could also be complex issues of international law to be dealt with.

A further divergence in trade policy is reflected in the choice of following a more autarchic, import-substituting strategy or one that is more open and 'free market'. The smaller GCC states have generally followed the latter strategy and reflecting this preference, Bahrain, Kuwait, Qatar and the UAE became founding members of the WTO when it was launched in January 1995; Oman also joined in 2002. However, after a decade of protracted negotiations, Saudi Arabia only joined in 2005. Indeed it has been argued that the relatively low intra-regional trade volumes between Saudi Arabia and most other GCC states (excluding Bahrain) could be attributable to the pursuit of conflicting development strategies (Looney 2003). While Saudi Arabia has historically pursued import substitution policies (predominantly in the agricultural sector) in an attempt to become more self-sufficient, the UAE, for example, has followed a far more open and 'free market' approach to trade focusing on maximizing its comparative advantages and creating a thriving re-export industry.

Investment policy

As a further dimension of their willingness to 'open up' their economies to the forces of globalization, the smaller GCC states, in particular Bahrain, Oman and the UAE, have been keen to liberalize and open up their economies to foreign investment at a much faster pace than Saudi Arabia. With Bahrain and Oman the logic probably lies in their limited oil reserves, as Kuwait, another small state but with ample oil reserves, is less open and in this sense similar to Saudi Arabia.

While Saudi Arabia has introduced some investment regulation reforms in recent years, such as cutting taxes on foreign investors from 45 per cent to 20 per cent in 2003, outside of the hydrocarbon sector Saudi Arabia cannot compete at present with Bahrain, Qatar or the UAE in terms of attracting FDI. The latter have implemented many reforms so as to create a favourable infrastructure and environment for foreign investors. Additionally, the Kingdom's deeply conservative society and the restrictions on some personal freedoms make it a much less attractive place for multinationals in which to locate their regional headquarters.

As was mentioned in Chapter 2, the UAE has been particularly successful in attracting FDI contributing to its fast pace of growth in recent years. In 2005 across the GCC the measure of FDI as a proportion of GDP was highest in the UAE at 9.3 per cent, followed by Bahrain at 7.8 per cent compared with only 1.5 per cent in Saudi Arabia. The UAE's success in this respect can be attributed in part to economic liberalization in the field of foreign investment regulation in particular that of creating several FTZs which provide incentives for foreign companies to establish themselves, such as allowing 100 per cent foreign ownership and full profit repatriation.

For example the Jebel Ali FTZ, established in 1985 by the Dubai government, has attracted more than 1,600 businesses from over 85 countries, many of which are multinationals (ESCWA 2001). This policy – attracting significant FDI to Dubai – has played a major part in the UAE becoming the de facto commercial and business hub not just of the GCC but the entire MENA region. Following Dubai's lead Qatar and Bahrain also have plans to set up a string of FTZs; indeed if we consider financial services in this bracket they already operate some – the Qatar Financial Centre and the Bahrain Financial Harbour.

Another significant difference is in terms of investment policy in the real estate sector. Many of the smaller GCC states have allowed foreigners to invest in property and in some instances actually own 'freehold rights' (99-year renewable leases in the case of Dubai). The UAE offers dozens of specified locations where non-GCC nationals can purchase property – as part of many packages residency is granted not just for the principle owner but also his/her family. Similar opportunities are also being offered by Oman and Qatar.

However, at the time of writing, these kinds of policy reform do not appear to be on the horizon in either Kuwait or Saudi Arabia. While it is probably understandable for these two countries to continue to exclude foreign multinationals from their upstream hydrocarbon sectors, their more restrictive attitude to other forms of foreign investment presents a sharp contrast to the policies of the other GCC states and may involve a painful re-adjustment if they are going to move towards the more open and welcoming approach which seems to be the growing tendency among their GCC neighbours. Here again, certain sectors within two of the GCC states may prove resistant to the economic costs which would fall upon them were these states to have to re-align their economic strategies in a direction consistent with those of the majority of GCC states – moreover a direction which is probably more consistent with the ultimate objective of MU and greater economic integration.

Labour nationalization policy

While the GCC have collectively agreed to address rising national unemployment levels through raising the cost of expatriate labour and replacing it with nationals in both the public and private sectors the extent to which these policies are being pursued is uneven. If these discrepancies persist countries which are implementing extensive labour nationalization programmes and enforcing them could end up at a commercial disadvantage with businesses seeking to relocate to GCC states which have less restrictive labour policies.

For example, in Bahrain and Saudi Arabia where unemployment rates are estimated to be as high as 13 and 15 per cent per cent respectively (UN 2002; EIU 2006a), the problem has become a social and political one and nationalization policies are being pursued quite rigorously. Saudi Arabia introduced various labour laws during the 1990s, one required private businesses employing more than 20 people to increase the number of Saudi nationals by five per cent annually. Another prevented businesses hiring expatriates for some administrative positions while another increased the fees involved in recruiting expatriates (Looney 2004). In contrast, in Kuwait, Qatar and the UAE, where the unemployment problem is much less pressing, nationalization policies are less vigorously pursued.

If GCC labour policies are not synchronized by the time MU comes into being the states with the most liberal labour laws are likely to see proportionately more inward investment. For if one member state requires a potential foreign investor to hire a certain percentage of nationals irrespective of wage demand and skills set and another member state does not, the latter would clearly be at a competitive advantage. Indeed, some Saudi businessmen are concerned that if the Saudization policy continues to be expanded and rigorously applied it will cause a brain-drain to neighbouring financial and commercial centres such as Dubai (Looney 2004).

Fiscal convergence criteria

The adoption and enforcement of fiscal rules is important in order to avoid contagion – in this case, fiscal indiscipline in one member state spilling over to others. Some form of safeguard will be important for the GCC because if a given member state runs excessive and consecutive deficits it will need to fund this by borrowing more. But by doing so it will put upward pressure on interest rates, which in turn would make it more expensive for other members to borrow or pay down their existing liabilities.

Arguably once a member of the MU there will be less incentive for fiscally loose states to control their spending as their fiscal irresponsibility will be borne by the group as a whole. Post-2010, Kuwait for instance, could find itself a victim of 'free-riding' where other members take advantage of its strong fiscal discipline in order to spend more freely themselves. Kuwait unlike most other GCC states has not experienced a fiscal deficit since oil prices hit their nadir in 1998. Unsustainable budgetary positions (continually borrowing to cover expenditure when oil prices are low) increase the risk of debt default or debt monetization (printing more money), both of which could jeopardize the future GCC MU.

As was established in Chapter 4, according to the GCC Monetary Union Unit at the Secretariat the region's finance ministers have agreed to adopt fiscal rules broadly similar to the fiscal criteria embodied in EMU's SGP. However, some economists have felt the SGP diverted attention away from important structural reforms, therefore harming European growth prospects and condemning it to 'a low – level equilibrium trap' (Eichengreen and Wyplosz 1998).

The GCC, by adopting and implementing fiscal rules designed for industrialized and diversified economies could therefore impede their own structural development and impose unacceptable economic and social costs upon their populations. The Eurozone economies are developed and diversified economies where limitations on public debt to GDP can be justified. However, public debt is not necessarily a bad thing for transitional economies so long as the borrowed capital is being used to invest in income-generating industries. If a European-style debt rule is imposed which does not distinguish between borrowing to spend and borrowing to invest then member states which wish to issue debt to fund their future economic development and diversification may be unfairly penalized (Rutledge 2008a). The GCC must therefore ensure the fiscal rules they adopt factor in both the historically volatile price of oil and a serious consideration of the fact that the GCC economies are at a stage of economic development which is quite distinct from that enjoyed by the European nations at the time of their MU. In other words, while it is clear that entering into MU without an agreed set of fiscal rules would be potentially very costly for the GCC, it is also clear that the fiscal criteria need to be tailored to the bloc's economic characteristics, as inappropriate rules are also likely to be costly.

As of December 2007, apart from agreeing to meet and discuss any potential future breaches of fiscal discipline, GCC leaders have thus far not decided upon the precise mechanisms by which fiscal discipline rules would be enforced. As Saudi Arabia has been the main violator of the fiscal debt to GDP rule, it is hard to see without predefined and collectively agreed enforcement mechanisms, how the smaller states could ensure Saudi compliance. Here again, therefore, is an area of macroeconomic policy where the pursuit of the collective objective of MU and greater economic integration must be flexible enough to recognize that a 'one size fits all' approach does not impose unacceptable costs on one or more candidates, a consideration which is all the more important, given that it is the GCC's largest and most influential member which would probably bear the brunt of such an intransigent approach.

Political 'costs'

In addition to the potential economic costs which individual GCC states might incur as they move towards MU, we must also acknowledge that there exists a broad category of political costs which, at least for certain states, could prove even more daunting for their leaders than the purely economic ones. Many of these costs will either accrue to certain groups within the GCC such as the ruling elites or they may be unevenly distributed across the bloc and will be bigger for some GCC states than for others. For instance, Saudi Arabian businesses may press the government to relinquish, the many, pervasive levers of state control over the economy so as to enable the Saudi private sector to remain competitive vis-à-vis its more liberal neighbours. Yet such pressures may be resisted in some quarters of the Kingdom. Indeed, the MU project itself may be viewed by these dominant, socially conservative elements as a Trojan horse, heralding in not only greater economic liberalization but also greater personal freedoms and 'Western' values.

Similarly, and particularly, in the current climate of high oil prices, the GCC states may be less concerned over the economic cost implications of adopting and adhering to fiscal discipline rules as they are with the associated political 'costs'. If clear fiscal rules (whether 'Maastricht type' or otherwise) are officially adopted in the lead-up to MU, then assessing compliance to these will require improved budget reporting and much greater fiscal transparency. However, in certain states, where budget transparency is poor, this may be viewed as an unwelcome intrusion into what has hitherto been considered a largely private matter under the control of the national elites. In fact, Mundell (1997) argued that wanting to protect the secrecy of national statistics might be a strong *disincentive* to joining an MU.

Indeed, here there is a rather dangerous overlap between what might appear to be genuine economic arguments and self-seeking political motives on the part of certain elites. For example, 'fiscal sovereignty' arguments could be used as an excuse for the perpetuation of practices which are inimical to the transparency and honesty which are themselves a prerequisite of a successful MU. In this context it should be emphasized that statistics have political resonance the world over but possibly even more so for 'rentier states'. A senior GCC Secretariat official, Abdelaziz Al-Uwaisheg, Director of the Economic Integration Department, commented on the issue saying 'we have different levels in the GCC. Oman, Bahrain and Kuwait have high levels of transparency … the others are working on it' (*Gulf Times* 2004).

GCC economic data transparency is often patchy and the legislative supervision of spending by the ruling families is in places insufficient. For example, in 2002 an IMF report estimated that 20 per cent of Saudi Arabia's oil receipts were not acknowledged in the government budget of 2000 (Khalaf 2002). The UAE has also been encouraged by the IMF to improve its budget reporting. For most of the period of analysis the official UAE budget has recorded consecutive budget deficits. While in reality the UAE's fiscal deficits are more than covered by overseas investment income, it still means a lot of income is off-budget.[1]

Such opaque budget reporting may be considered as unacceptable to other more transparent prospective MU members. Unless all the prospective MU members agree to greater public scrutiny of their national budgets and adopt the same statistical standards (in order to create comparable statistics essential for making the optimal monetary policy decisions) the potential for fiscal 'free-riding' within the MU will be ever present. Inevitably such 'free-riding' will appear as a significant cost to those states 'carrying the riders' and as such can only be expected to slow down and perhaps even bring to a halt the progression towards MU.

There are also issues of 'political cost' arising from the requirement to establish supra-national economic institutions in the lead-up to full MU, in particular a GCC central bank and GCC statistical agency. This issue has the potential to become politically controversial given that the standards and integrity of existing sovereign institutions will be pooled into one. If the new institution only reflects the mean of the five existing central banks and monetary authorities, some states may feel they are downgrading their existing standards – a cost they may well feel unwilling to pay. And there are certainly grounds for concern on this score. The World Bank's Governance and Anti-Corruption Index provides a rating of the level of a nation's governance and institutional quality obtained through surveys with experts, businesses and individuals across the GCC (Kaufmann *et al.* 2007). In particular two indicators can reveal the differences in institutional quality across the GCC: 'regulatory quality' which measures the ability of the government to formulate and implement appropriate regulations that promote private sector development and 'government effectiveness' which measures the quality of public services and institutions and the degree of independence from political pressures. According to the above indices the UAE, despite being a federal state, receives the highest rating for both indicators Bahrain and Qatar come next in terms of regulatory quality and government effectiveness respectively. Yet, the institutional quality of the bloc's largest economy, Saudi Arabia, is ranked the lowest in terms of both regulatory quality and government effectiveness (see Figure 5.2).

Clearly Bahrain, Qatar and the UAE have achieved a high level of institutional credibility. The Bahrain monetary authority (BMA), for example, which is regarded by many as the region's best financial regulator, has considerable international kudos and has effectively managed what has until recently been the Arabian Peninsula's financial hub for much of the period of analysis. Unless the new GCC institutions are considered to be comparable or an improvement on their incumbents then these states in particular may be unwilling to cede decision-making powers to it.

In this respect the mandate of the future GCC central bank will be critical, as will, albeit to a lesser extent, the location of the new institutions. Just as the ECB inherited the institutional credibility and reputation of Germany's Bundesbank

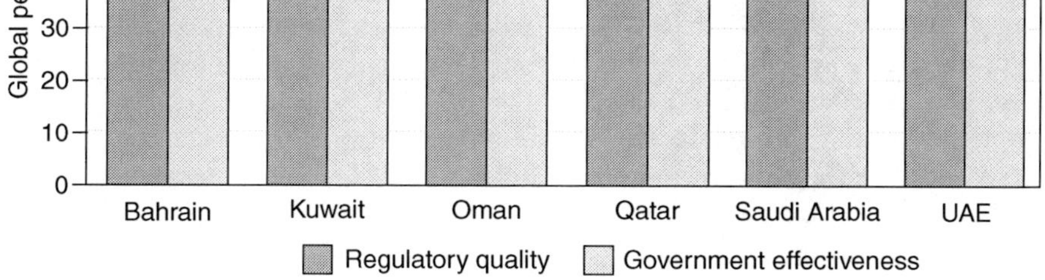

Figure 5.2 Institutional and regulatory quality rankings, 2006 (source: Adapted from Kaufmann *et al.* (2007)).

Note
The worldwide governance indicators project indexes 212 countries, 90th–100th Percentile being the best and 0th–10th percentile being the worst.

and is located in Frankfurt, so the embryonic GCC central bank may also inherit the institutional standards of the national predecessor. Hence locating the new central bank in Bahrain may well be optimal (but unlikely) and locating it in Riyadh would be less optimal (but quite likely). The UAE – being the region's second biggest economy and with Dubai now vying for Bahrain's crown as the Arabian Peninsula's premier financial hub – may end up the compromise candidate. Indeed, other central banks in the region also appear to favour the UAE as a 'safe' location, in 2004 the Kuwaiti Finance Minister, Mahmud Al-Nuri, told reporters that the GCC central bank would be located in the UAE (*Khaleej Times* 2004), although since then there has been no definitive confirmation of this.

Finally, any consideration of the political costs of establishing a GCC MU cannot avoid a discussion of questions of regional power and geo-strategic dominance. Saudi Arabia is by far the largest and most important state in the region. The Kingdom accounts for approximately 48 per cent of the region's GDP and is home to 66 per cent of its population; in 1981 it hosted the meeting which led to the creation of the GCC (Cordesman 2003) and has hosted the GCC Secretariat in its capital ever since. While Saudi Arabia's participation in the GCC MU would dramatically increase the market size for the other members they may also consider being even more closely tied to the Kingdom as potentially costly – costly in terms of their likely subordination to Saudi monetary policy preferences, in terms of the Kingdom wanting to steer future joint economic policy to suit its own domestic economy and, finally, the possibility that social and political tensions existent in the Kingdom may spill over.

As Mundell states, 'broadly speaking, Saudi Arabia will wield palpable influence because it cannot be expected that the other GCC states will put forward fiscal and monetary policies that would go utterly counter to Saudi Arabia's interests' (Mundell quoted in Al-Hajji 1999). It may therefore be inevitable that the smaller economies offer Saudi Arabia a proportionately large role in determining the region's post-MU monetary policies. Whether this would be seen as a necessary and worthwhile cost to bear in order to gain unfettered access to the Kingdom's large consumer market, or whether it would appear a burden just too onerous to accept, remains unclear at the time of writing.

One particular concern for the smaller states and hence their willingness to enter into an MU with Saudi Arabia is that the latter might attempt to use the project as a vehicle for exercising not only economic dominance over them but also political leverage. For example Legrenzi (2002) has argued that concerns over Saudi Arabian dominance has been a significant factor which has led the other GCC states to move at only a sluggish pace towards greater integration. Along with unresolved territorial disputes,[2] relations between Saudi Arabia and some of the smaller GCC states have certainly been strained in recent years. For example the Kingdom's very public disquiet with Bahrain over its decision to sign an FTA with the US (although it could be argued that such disquiet was entirely justified given that it was a serious blow to MU) and a souring of relations between Saudi Arabia and Qatar over the latter's state-controlled Al Jazeera news channel which has criticized the Saudi regime.

Political instability within the Kingdom itself is also likely to be of concern to its more affluent and stable neighbours. Mundell (1997) has argued that joining an MU with a politically unstable neighbour would be considered as a disincentive by other prospective members. The emergence of militant groups in Saudi Arabia since 2001 has raised real concerns over the stability of the country. The World Bank rates Saudi Arabia's political stability as the lowest in the GCC at just 26 percentile rank and this ranking has fallen from 51.5 since 1998 (see Figure 5.3).

For the likes of Qatar and the UAE, where political stability is far higher, the potentially adverse consequences of joining an MU dominated by Saudi Arabia could well be seen as a serious cost. While to date the terrorist attacks in the Kingdom do not appear to have reduced economic confidence in the UAE or, for example, the attractiveness of Dubai as a tourist destination and magnet for FDI, once joined together in MU, not only economic ties but also political relationships may become more interlinked and any political instability in one member state could thus be more contagious than at present. Even if this were not, in reality, a significant issue, the perception of such a possibility among Western investors and tourists might be seen as a serious risk, notably by the Emirati authorities who might fear that Dubai, as part of the 'Gulf dinar zone', might come to be viewed as part of the 'unstable Saudi Kingdom'.

It should be clear from the forgoing analysis that forming a GCC MU is by no means a cost-free exercise. Some of these costs are real in the sense that they will require sometimes difficult and painful adjustments. Others are more in the nature of fears and anxieties which may well prove to be ill-founded. Fortunately, as we describe in the next chapter, there are some very considerable economic, social and political gains to be had from pressing ahead with MU in a determined fashion.

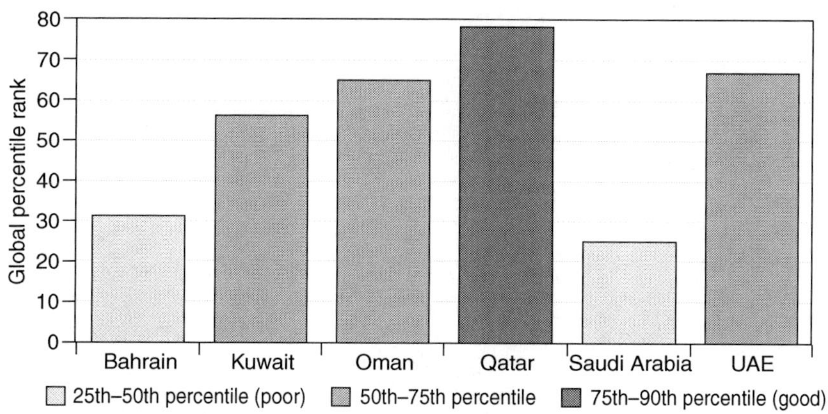

Figure 5.3 Political stability rankings, 2006 (source: Adapted from Kaufmann *et al.* (2007)).

Note
The worldwide governance indicators project indexes 212 countries, 90th–100th Percentile being the best and 0th–10th Percentile being the worst.

6 Potential benefits of GCC monetary union

The benefits of MU – both direct and indirect – are potentially considerable. They include: a reduction in transaction costs and exchange rate risk; increased levels of trade; better price transparency; economies of scale; an improved business climate; and the strengthening of capital markets. These *economic* benefits are covered in the first section of this chapter. However, MU also has the potential to act as a catalyst for a wider range of reforms and as a means to strengthen the bloc's international bargaining power. These issues are covered in the second section of this chapter under the title *associated* benefits.

As with the Eurozone many (microeconomic) benefits will be directly attributable to the introduction of the MU – efficiency gains through a reduction in transaction costs and the elimination of exchange rate uncertainty – others, resulting from complimentary reforms and prerequisite preparations, will be indirect. In certain instances such distinctions are hard to make, the GCC common market is illustrative of this. While the benefits from such a market would occur irrespective of MU per se, GCC leaders may only find the political will to establish one if deemed a necessary prerequisite for MU.

Furthermore, some benefits – such as increasing levels of intra-GCC trade – may take years if not decades to become appreciable and others will not only be contingent on the level of preparations taken prior to the launch of the Gulf dinar (see Chapter 4) but also on the nature of the MU the region decides to adopt (see Chapter 8).

On balance, we believe that if the participating GCC states undertake the necessary MU preparations there will be net benefits for the bloc as a whole. At the very least a successfully launched Gulf dinar would send a strong signal that the Gulf is a stable economic region and able to act cohesively as a unified monetary bloc. This, in turn, should result in strengthening domestic business confidence and encouraging longer term investments as well as attracting FDI inflows. It is worth reiterating, however, that as many of the benefits are contingent on the prerequisite reforms taking place, without these MU will undoubtedly be less advantageous.

The potential efficiency gains from the MU are likely to be marginal at first, as intra-GCC trade (even as a percentage of non-oil trade) is low if compared to Eurozone trade prior to the euro. Although the single currency is expected to promote intra-GCC trade, businesses see other micro- level factors to be more important obstacles to their growth prospects. The simplification of red tape and harmonization of business regulations are, in our view, necessary reforms that need take place if the potential intra-GCC trade gains from the single currency are to be realized.

The small size of many of the GCC economies suggests that they will see substantial benefits from access to a larger market, as it will allow them to exploit economies of scale. According to GCC business survey findings a majority of businesses are positive about the potential impact of MU on their businesses and consider new business opportunities to be a significant benefit of MU. With new business opportunities increased levels of intra-GCC competition are also likely to occur and although in the short run this could lead to adjustment costs, in the long run it will strengthen and improve the efficiency of businesses possibly leading to welfare gains for GCC consumers in the form of lower prices.

Nevertheless, the realization of such gains will be contingent, to no small degree, on their first being a fully functioning common market in place and, as will become apparent in this chapter, we attach considerable importance to this key prerequisite for MU. The potential gains from increasing price transparency acting to reduce price discrimination between GCC states will only come about if there is increased arbitrage between markets. At the same time the benefits of economies of scale and increasing competition will also be contingent on the completion of the common market.

We contend that GCC capital markets stand to benefit considerably from the planned MU, in particular the region's equity and emerging Islamic bond markets. The post-MU removal of exchange rate risk and reduction in liquidity risk may well lead to a lower cost of capital for businesses across the bloc and subsequently generate increasing issuance of financial instruments. Broader capital markets should create greater diversification opportunities for regional portfolios attracting greater levels of capital into increasing numbers of pan-GCC assets.

An important associated benefit of MU will be its potential to act as a catalyst for broader economic reform. The launch of a single currency will, as mentioned in Chapter 4, require a range of policy reforms and although these may prove to be demanding for certain governments they should be surmountable. The GCC leaders may be willing to take the opportunity to implement the policy prerequisites if they fully consider the long- term economic gains such reforms will generate, such as strengthening private sector confidence, increasing capital inflows and FDI, stabilizing macroeconomic cycles and improving regional stability and accountability.

Finally, a successful GCC MU could act to strengthen the bloc not only economically but also politically. On aggregate the GCC states will have a much stronger voice in international disputes and negotiations which should expand their influence on the global stage. A unified regional bloc acting with one voice, and one currency, could also give the views of the GCC states greater weight in terms of US and EU foreign policy towards the Middle East.

Such associated benefits, if fully appreciated, could increase the levels of political motivation towards the MU project. Further potential benefits stemming from post-MU policy choices such as the Gulf dinar becoming an independent currency, taking on a wider role and emerging as a regional anchorage and reserve currency will be considered in Chapter 8.

Economic benefits

Many of the likely economic benefits should arise through efficiency gains by way of reduced transaction costs and the elimination of exchange rate risk and uncertainty. In time these cost reductions should lead to an increase in levels of intra-regional trade, investment, tourism and services integration. While the magnitude of these efficiency gains will be initially contingent on the level of existing intra-regional trade, empirical research (Rose 1999; Frankel and Rose 2000; Fielding and Shields 2005) suggests that members of an MU are likely to see substantial increases over time.

Access to an enlarged market will allow businesses to exploit economies of scale and at the same time increased competition will lead to downward pressure on prices. The single currency will allow for greater price transparency as the prices of like-for-like goods and services across the bloc will be easily comparable. This should lead to fewer opportunities for price discrimination between GCC markets and concomitant gains for GCC consumers.

The potential impact of MU on GCC business expectations may have important implications for investment decisions and thus macroeconomic growth. Furthermore, the introduction of the Gulf dinar should help allocate capital more efficiently and provide greater financing opportunities for the region's emerging private sector. Eventually, the microeconomic efficiency gains from forming an MU will translate into macroeconomic gains through increases in investment and thus output.

The gains for trade

At face value intra-GCC trade, at less than 7.9 per cent of total imports, is low especially when compared to Eurozone trade prior to 1999, although if oil is factored out, as argued in Chapter 3, the figure is somewhat more impressive; amounting to 16.3 per cent of total exports in 2003. Ideally, we would measure the aggregate potential savings from the removal of these micro-level costs, but in the absence of aggregate bank data on GCC exchange rate transactions, it is not possible to do so. In the case of EMU the savings for businesses through the removal of exchange rate-related transaction costs was estimated to be equal to 0.4 per cent of GDP. It is therefore safe to say that the savings for the GCC economies are likely to be smaller given the lower levels of intra-GCC trade. This would suggest that the reduction of transaction costs and exchange rate risk on existing intra-GCC trade will, in the short run at least, bring about only limited benefits for the GCC economies.

However, as the bloc collectively moves to diversify through expanding its non-oil trade any policy which facilitates this must be seen in a positive light. Furthermore, the GCC business survey sample indicated that a large proportion of businesses, in particular SMEs, have strong trading links with other GCC states. SMEs constitute the largest segment of the GCC business community and the burden of currency-related transaction costs weighs heavier upon them than upon larger companies (Commission of the European Communities 1990). This suggests that MU, by eliminating the exchange rate-related transaction costs for a significant number of SMEs should be beneficial for these businesses and given the latters' weight in the regional economy, for GCC business as a whole.

Overall, the majority of GCC business survey respondents, 84 per cent,[1] thought that the MU would provide some micro-level benefits (Rutledge 2008b), with the removal of exchange rate risk and new business opportunities thought to be of greatest potential benefit. While exchange rate risk between GCC states has been limited due to the fixed dollar pegs uncertainties still remain. In recent years there has been increasing speculation over the region's exchange rate choices in the private sector with large bets on currency appreciation.[2] A hard fix in the form of MU would eliminate exchange rate risk altogether removing hedging costs on transactions with other firms within the currency area and reducing uncertainty associated with the existence of national currencies and exchange rate policies (Bris *et al.* 2002).

Despite the fact that GCC businesses acknowledged the potential benefits of eliminating exchange rate risk, they did not consider currency and exchange rate issues to be very important when asked about factors limiting their growth. Factors other than exchange rate-related costs were felt to be more important: 34 per cent of business respondents chose 'restrictive regulations' followed by 16 per cent choosing 'lack of skilled labour', only 6.6 per cent of respondents chose 'exchange rate-related costs' (see Table 6.1). This finding suggests that the simplification of bureaucratic formalities and harmonization of business regulations across the GCC are complementary reforms which should take place as part of the process of building a common market and MU. Indeed, even though monetary policy issues do not rank very highly among contemporary business

Table 6.1 Obstacles to growth, GCC Business Survey

Potential obstacle	*Frequency (%)*
Restrictive regulations	33.9
Lack of skilled labour	15.9
Lack of clear property rights	14.1
Protective tariffs and quotas	14.1
Lack of access to credit	14.1
Exchange rate related costs	6.6
Other obstacles	1.3

Source: Rutledge (2008b).

concerns, there is nevertheless solid support for policies that would reduce exchange rate risks, in other words the MU project.

Considerable evidence suggests that there are dynamic trade gains arising from MU which we should also consider. Empirical research by Rose (1999) suggests that MU could triple bilateral trade between member states. While Rose's results were considered somewhat controversial several modifications of the 'gravity' model were undertaken and the results were considered to be robust. Rose, however, points out that the model gives no indication of the causal direction between increasing trade and MU and it may be that MU comes about as the result of large bilateral trade flows and not vice versa.

However, there is no shortage of evidence pointing to a positive relationship between the establishment of MU and the expansion of trade. For example, empirical evidence suggests that in Europe the effect on trade of the introduction of a common currency has been significant (Baldwin and Wyplosz 2006). An analysis of the French franc zones also shows 'strong evidence that … membership has promoted higher trade volumes in the past than could otherwise have been expected' (Fielding and Shields 2005: 700). Such evidence of a positive single currency effect on trade has arguably increased the attractiveness of MU for the GCC and could potentially provide an important indirect benefit for the region. Increasing intra-regional trade will undoubtedly be a bonus to the GCC states given that it is mostly non-oil trade and a key policy objective is to diversify export revenues away from hydrocarbons.

Further benefits are also likely to arise from the transaction cost savings on intra-GCC capital flows, tourism and travel, which are likely to be facilitated by the launch of a single currency. While it is difficult to calculate these gains empirically, such savings are likely to have a positive economic impact particularly for those GCC states which have already diversified into tourism and banking and finance, such as Bahrain, Oman and the UAE who stand to gain relatively more in this respect than would Kuwait or Saudi Arabia.

Price transparency and convergence

A single GCC currency will allow for direct comparison between the prices of like-for-like goods across the GCC markets thus making price discrimination much more difficult for producers. Price discrimination occurs because of segmentation between markets brought about, in part, by the existence of different national currencies (Engle and Rogers 1995). In light of extensive intra-GCC tourism and travel, post-MU any price disparities will become increasingly obvious to consumers. Eventually this price transparency should lead to convergence in the prices of tradable goods or PPP across the bloc. Persistent deviations in PPP can distort efficient resource allocation across the region and penalizes customers in those GCC states where prices are higher. However, post-MU price convergence can only occur if there is unfettered arbitrage in the goods markets and if there are no other significant transaction costs to businesses involved in the trading of goods between member states.

Previous research has shown that past deviations from PPP have been persistent in the GCC due to years of fixed nominal exchange rates, periods of high dollar volatility and significantly – weak arbitrage in the goods markets (Hassanain 2004). Moreover, when businesses were asked whether they expected to charge the same price for identical goods across the region after the introduction of the single currency the respondents were equally split (see Figure 6.1).

Those business respondents that said they wouldn't charge the same price for their goods cited 'varying operating costs' most frequently as their reason such as differences in local taxes, fees, overhead and distribution costs. This finding suggests that eliminating the cost of buying and selling foreign currencies is not the only significant source of transaction costs for businesses which might lead to price divergence across the bloc.

Evidence from other MUs has also illustrated that the convergence of prices post-MU across member states is often contingent on the presence, or otherwise, of other transaction costs. Engle and Rogers (1995) considered the border between the US and Canada and found evidence that the further the distance between cities the greater the difference between the price of an identical good. Research focusing on the CFA French franc zone and the ECCU has also shown that geographical characteristics are an important factor in determining the size of transaction costs such as distribution costs (Fielding and Shields 2005).

Regardless of the geographical characteristics of the GCC, if consumers are to benefit from equality of prices following MU, an essential prerequisite is the establishment of a common market allowing for effective goods markets arbitrage and the removal of non-exchange rate-related transaction costs. Indeed, in

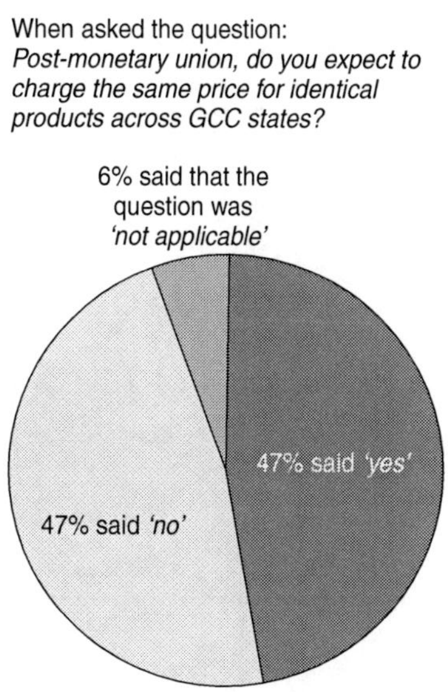

Figure 6.1 Impact of MU on price discrimination, GCC Business Survey (source: Rutledge (2007)).

the case of EMU it was found that the bulk of price convergence across member states occurred following the completion of the single market, rather than after the launch of the common currency (Rogers 2002).

Economies of scale and increased competition

It has been argued that small and open economies tend to benefit more from forming an MU because their currencies and markets are marginal and a single currency enables them to take advantage of the full benefits of the larger, common market (McKinnon 1963). It is also true that post-EMU it was the relatively smaller member economies such as Ireland and Portugal which saw particularly impressive rates of economic growth. The smaller GCC economies may therefore benefit from MU more in this regard than would Saudi Arabia. Bahraini and Qatari businesses, for example, currently have domestic markets of 749,000 and 839,000 consumers respectively and would gain considerably from access to Saudi Arabia's market of 23.7 million potential new consumers providing considerable economies of scale to be exploited.

Survey findings have indicated that firms consider new business opportunities to be a significant benefit of MU (Rutledge 2008b). When they were asked which GCC state they considered to offer the greatest potential for new commercial opportunities following the launch of the MU, the UAE, the second largest economy in the region, was most frequently chosen with 34 per cent of business respondents choosing this state followed closely by 30 per cent choosing Saudi Arabia (see Table 6.2). Geographical proximities as well as market size seemed, understandably, to influence responses, specifically Bahraini and Kuwaiti businesses felt that Saudi Arabia would offer them the most new business opportunities whereas Omani businesses considered the UAE best placed in this respect.

Table 6.2 Greatest potential for new business opportunities post-MU (%)

Business	*Greatest potential opportunity in:*					
	Bahrain	*Kuwait*	*Oman*	*Qatar*	*KSA*	*UAE*
Bahraini	9.5	0.0	4.8	23.8	47.6	14.3
Kuwaiti	6.5	12.9	3.2	12.9	32.3	32.3
Omani	0.0	5.6	16.7	15.9	25.0	44.4
Qatari	12.5	0.0	12.5	37.5	12.5	25.0
Saudi	0.0	6.2	12.4	15.9	34.5	31.0
Emirati	3.1	5.2	3.1	26.8	23.7	38.1
Total[a]	2.6	5.9	8.5	19.3	30.1	33.7

Source: Rutledge (2007).

Note

a This total reflects the perceived opportunities of investing in a given economy post-MU, the UAE having the greatest and Bahrain having the least. Figures underlined demonstrate the home state as offering the best potential for new business opportunities.

These results indicate that although Saudi Arabia offers a significant enlargement of the potential market for smaller GCC states nevertheless the business environment in the UAE is clearly considered more inviting.

In the long run the establishment of a common market should allow for greater competition between GCC private sector businesses as they seek to expand their operations in new markets across the bloc. Eventually through a process of mergers and acquisitions (M&A) larger and more efficient GCC businesses may emerge that are better equipped to deal with global competitors, which as WTO members they will inevitably face. However, in the short run such restructuring maybe a painful process with some inefficient businesses used to operating in a relatively sheltered environment suffering the most. Businesses in Saudi Arabia – already operating in a relatively larger market – are more likely to be able to adapt to a more competitive business climate, while those in smaller GCC states such as Bahrain and Qatar may face greater adjustment costs initially.

Increased competition in Europe in the lead-up to MU and during its aftermath led to a substantial increase in M&A activities. Prior to 1997 the number of M&As in Europe had been about 10,000 per year but post-1997 this figure began to rise rapidly and by 2000 the annual number of M&As amounted to 12,557 operations (Baldwin and Wyplosz 2006) Two-thirds of all M&A activity in Europe that took place in this period was in the service sector, a sector which has seen substantial growth in the GCC since the beginning of the current oil price boom.

In particular M&A activity in Europe's banking sector grew at an unprecedented rate, having a major impact on bank restructuring and eventually leading to the emergence of international banking firms and networks (Danthine *et al.* 2000). So far M&A activity in the GCC banking sector has been very weak. However, pressure from WTO rules to allow foreign competition in the banking sector is leading to some consolidation in the GCC national banking sectors. For example in the UAE in 2007 the merger of the National Bank of Dubai and Emirates Bank was announced and, according to its Chairman, Ahmad Al-Tayer, the bank has aggressive plans for further intra-regional acquisitions 'the time has come for [intra regional] bank mergers. With large assets and equity base, we are looking at regional expansion' (Bowman 2007).

The long-term benefits to GCC businesses and consumers from increased competition will, however, be dependent upon there being a level playing field for the region's businesses in all national markets. In this respect existing national credit policies which seek to stimulate investment in certain sectors through the provision of subsidized government loans or state aid to national businesses will be distortive and threaten the potential long-term benefits which may be gained. Whether the GCC governments are prepared to liberalize their credit policies and adopt European-style legislation which prohibits state aid will ultimately require a substantial degree of political will. Competition laws will also have to be strengthened across the bloc otherwise there could be future disputes and subsidization will create unfair advantages.

Business climate and investment

Private sector expectations about price stability and monetary credibility are crucial in determining future investments and thus macroeconomic growth. Therefore the expectations of GCC businesses regarding the MU are likely to have important implications for future economic growth.

Although, as we have established, survey results suggest that companies do not currently rank exchange rate issues very important to their businesses, businesses can be expected to respond favourably to the MU as business survey findings indicate a general optimism in the business community at the macro-level regarding the future MU (Rutledge 2008b). The majority of businesses – 76 per cent – felt 'very optimistic' or 'optimistic' about its likely success.[3] Only five per cent of businesses sampled were 'pessimistic' or 'very pessimistic' (see Figure 6.2).

Businesses were also optimistic about the MU when it came to their own prospects. When asked specifically how they thought the single currency would affect them, more than three-quarters of business respondents said that they thought the effect would be 'positive' or 'very positive'.[4] Only two per cent of respondents thought that the effect of MU would be 'negative' or 'very negative' (see Figure 6.2). From this result it would be fair to say that overall GCC businesses appear to think that MU will be a 'positive thing' but as we have seen consider other factors to be of greater priority – some of which should however be addressed by the establishment of the common market (see Table 6.1).

Overall, it is fair to say that GCC businesses are confident about the expected success of the GCC MU and are optimistic about the likely effect it will have on their businesses. This finding bodes well for investment trends and thus growth in the GCC economies during the transition period to MU. Nevertheless, the gains to the business community will, as is the case with other benefits, depend on whether or not the policy prerequisites are made in advance. Preparing businesses and households for the Gulf dinar will be critical in reducing uncertainty and supporting economic confidence (see Chapter 4).

Capital market growth

Through the removal of national obstacles to capital movement, exchange rate risks and transaction costs it is assumed that capital can move unhindered in seeking out the highest returns and thus capital allocation across the bloc will be more efficient. Increased transparency of asset prices and returns should also allow for a better comparison of share price performance across the bloc providing investors with important signals about where the most productive investment opportunities lie. The reduction of the aforementioned risks, along with lower liquidity risk from deeper capital market integration, should lower the cost of capital for businesses encouraging investment and consequently will be beneficial for economic growth overall. Ultimately therefore the benefits that accrue to the GCC's capital markets are likely to be felt beyond the financial sector (King and Levine 1993).

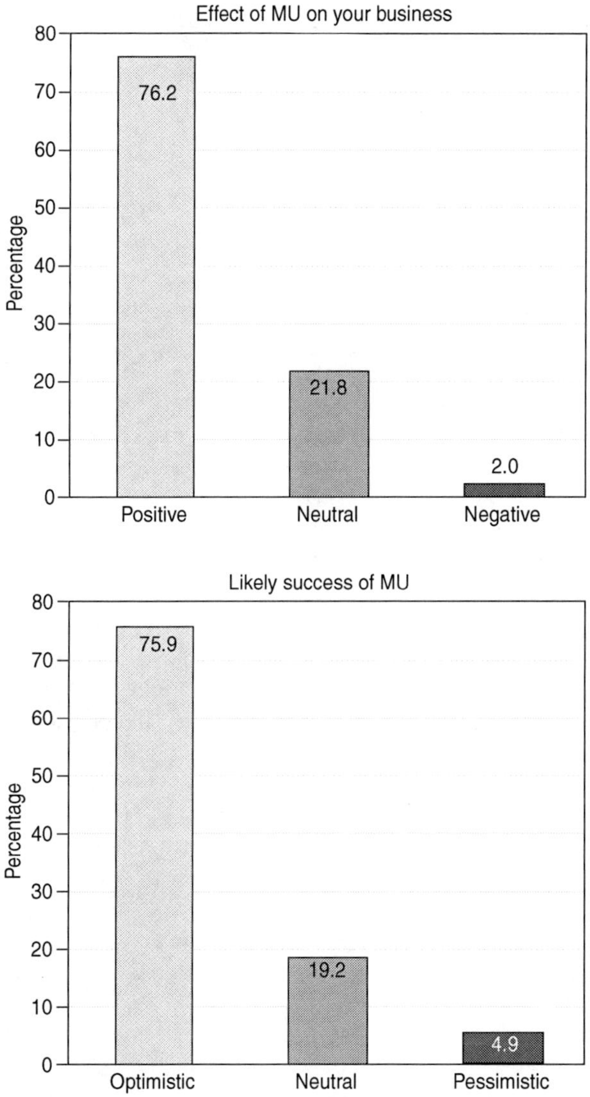

Figure 6.2 Business expectations of MU, GCC Business Survey (source: Rutledge (2008b)).

Integration between the relatively segmented GCC financial markets is a process which has been occurring gradually over the period of study although the pace has quickened in the past few years with the ratification of capital market provisions laid out in Article Five of the GCC Economic Agreement of 2001 (see Chapter 3). Yet despite recent GCC capital market expansion – with aggregate stock market capitalization growing by over 500 per cent between

2000 and 2007 – these markets still suffer from limited depth and breadth of investments. The risks associated with these characteristics could be mitigated indirectly by the MU project.

Currently GCC markets suffer from significant liquidity risk. Compared to international stock markets, which typically have a turnover ratio of 90 to 170 per cent, those of the GCC markets are much lower averaging only 45 per cent in 2004 (Al-Sadik 2006). Furthermore, despite increasing numbers of IPOs the breadth of GCC market listings remains limited. Across the GCC markets at the end of the first half of 2005 the top five stocks accounted for approximately 68 per cent of market capitalization in Oman, 62 per cent in Qatar, 61 per cent in Bahrain, 60 per cent in Saudi Arabia, 38 per cent in Kuwait and 37 per cent in the UAE (Al-Sadik 2006).

The launch of a single currency should help to reduce such risks and provide important gains operating through the enlargement and deepening of GCC financial markets. A fully integrated and enlarged GCC capital market with access to a broader base of regional investors should deepen liquidity, benefiting many of the small national markets. The reduced risk on cross border transactions will generate increased diversification options for regional investors and allow for the rebalancing of portfolios towards assets that may have previously been considered too risky (Danthine *et al.* 2000). Risk reduction should also lead to a lower cost of capital for businesses spurring market-based financing by businesses and increasing the breadth of these markets. Indeed evidence from EMU indicated that the single currency had lowered the cost of capital for firms inside the union relative to that of firms outside it which had led to increased issuance of financial instruments and corporate investment (Bris *et al.* 2002).

The single currency should also result in increasing competition between the GCC stock markets. Following the significant stock market corrections in the first quarter of 2006, the Saudi authorities announced they would turn the national stock market into a share holding company open to private involvement, seemingly to 'help the stock market operate on a more professional and transparent basis and introduce new products and services' (*Gulf Daily News* 2006). Greater competition for regional capital following the launch of the single currency might also lead to pressure for further improvements in the management and efficiency of other national stock markets.

The experience of the euro has illustrated that the financial sector can gain substantially from the introduction of a unified currency. According to Bernanke (2004) 'the most important benefit of the (European) currency union has been and will likely continue to be its strengthening of European financial markets'. The impact of the euro on European financial markets and corporate bond markets in particular, has been significant. Euro-denominated equity markets amounted to much more than the sum of aggregate national markets and corporate bond markets saw significant growth post-EMU. According to Galati and Tsatsaronis (2001) corporate debt issuance expanded substantially on the launch of the euro with the combined issuance of the corporate and financial sectors more than tripling since 1998 (Galati and Tsatsaronis 2001). The introduction of the euro, it is also thought, led to the lessening of other technical and regulatory constraints which had previously segmented European financial markets thus deepening the process of market integration (Galati and Tsatsaronis 2001).

We consider MU is likely to benefit the region's *sukuk* (Islamic bond) market considerably. Sturm and Siegfried (2005) estimate that GCC bond issues currently amount to less than an estimated three per cent of regional GDP. Nevertheless this market has grown significantly in recent years. As was the case with euro-denominated bonds, new bond issues in the Gulf dinar will most likely attract greater regional funds, as well as international capital. Depending on whether the Gulf dinar remains pegged to the dollar or not, it could become the currency of choice for the issuance of both GCC and non-GCC Islamic *sukuks*. With the launch of the unified GCC currency, the choice of issuing in the regional currency will be attractive for GCC governments and corporations in order to reduce any currency exposure. Presently most GCC bonds are issued in dollars, but recently First Islamic Investment Bank of Bahrain issued a *sukuk* in euros (Liquidity Management Centre 2007).

In order for the GCC financial sector to reap the full benefits of MU a number of accompanying reforms will be necessary not least the harmonization of banking and financial regulations. The removal of existing barriers to market integration, such as differences in national financial market legislation and auditing standards as well as other legal and fiscal obstacles will be advantageous and should be viewed as desirable (if not essential) complementary reforms in the MU process. Cooperation among national financial authorities in creating a regional financial services authority would assist in simplifying regulations for market participants and thus facilitate cross-border investments. The increased risks of financial contagion brought about by tighter integration will require improved supervision and better regulation of the GCC financial system to ensure its stability overall.

Associated benefits

The desire to establish an MU along the lines of EMU could prove to be an important catalyst for economic reform in the region. While achieving all the European criteria for MU (see Chapter 4) may initially prove to be demanding for the GCC, should they go some way towards meeting them, as they are undoubtedly attempting to do, then the process of establishing MU itself will bring important associated benefits. Indeed, the MU project could provide an opportune moment for the GCC states to initiate important and overdue reforms in accountability and transparency and to strengthen both their economic and political ties so as to emerge as a more cohesive and unified regional bloc.

A catalyst for reform

A host of associated benefits would no doubt arise if the following reforms took place as a part of the MU preparation process: the creation of strong supranational institutions such as a GCC central bank and a statistical agency, significant improvements in the availability and quality of statistical data, the timely dissemination of standardized economic statistics, greater fiscal discipline and more transparent and accountable budget reporting.

Improvements in the quality, standardization, coverage and timeliness of GCC statistical data are essential for managing the MU and in formulating effective monetary policy for the bloc (see Chapter 4). But in addition to this, better statistical reporting based on international standards will improve the effective functioning of markets and is likely to make the GCC, as an economic region more attractive to potential investors.

Adhering to fiscal discipline rules will prove important in ensuring the sustainability and coherence of the MU, but should also help ensure a more stable macroeconomic climate for these economies. In the past the highly cyclical nature of GCC government spending has often contributed to macroeconomic instability. The adoption of *appropriately designed* fiscal discipline rules should help to ensure a more balanced approach to government spending and encourage greater diversification of government sources of revenues. On top of these gains, strong fiscal discipline could lead to lower borrowing costs for the region and improve business confidence which should also help attract more FDI to the region. However, given that the GCC fiscal rules appear to be merely targets the degree to which they will be enforced is highly uncertain, yet without effective enforcement the rules may become meaningless and such reforms will be less likely to take place.

As was discussed in Chapter 4, MU will require a common scrutiny of fiscal budgets across the GCC as one country's fiscal health becomes a matter of concern to all member states. Greater pressure will come to bear on those GCC states, such as Saudi Arabia where off-balance sheet accounting seems to be common practice (Sender *et al.* 2007). Despite the fact that initially such reforms may be perceived as costly by some elements within GCC society, improvements in budget reporting and accountability will be immediately beneficial in building private sector confidence.

In particular, building the institutional infrastructure for MU will provide long-term benefits for the GCC states. At present the institutional structure of the GCC is relatively weak in terms of enforcing the implementation of GCC policy decisions. The delegation of power to autonomous pan-GCC institutions and technocrats should ensure greater accountability as well as bolstering the credibility of economic policy implementation.

We have already acknowledged (in Chapter 5) that such policy reforms may be perceived as costly to the region's ruling elites and therefore implementing them will undoubtedly require a strong political commitment to the process of integration. Nevertheless, for those GCC states striving to break away from dependence on hydrocarbons and the trappings of rentierism, the realization that such reforms will provide many long-lasting economic benefits as we have outlined above may provide sufficient motivation to forge ahead with them.

Strengthening the regional bloc

Another associated benefit of MU will be that the GCC becomes a stronger and more cohesive entity, acting with one powerful voice the GCC as a unified bloc may have greater influence in economic and political negotiations. On aggregate the GCC states, many of which have very small economic mass, will enjoy much greater bargaining power in international forums and negotiations than they would have done individually, especially in light of the global strategic significance of the regional bloc, sitting on two-fifths of global oil reserves.

The consensus among regional experts interviewed on the subject was that the MU will strengthen the GCC not just economically but also politically. The successful establishment of the MU will signify that the GCC countries have willingly sacrificed part of their sovereignty in order to achieve their goal of much deeper regional integration. Indeed forming a successful MU may strengthen feelings of solidarity and socio-political unity among its members, sentiments which may enhance the region's self-confidence and quite probably its international status.

At the very least MU should solidify the GCC as the dominant regional economic bloc and allow it to function more cohesively. While the pace of GCC regional integration in the past has been heavily criticized (Humayon and Presley 2001) it is nevertheless often cited as the most successful and resilient subregional Arab organization (Legrenzi 2002). When compared to the Arab league for instance, the GCC as a regional bloc is already considered to have achieved a meaningful level of integration. The successful establishment of the GCC MU will therefore be considered as a further indication of the bloc's regional strength. Conversely, if the GCC were to fail to achieve its goal of full economic integration in the form of MU then it could stand to lose considerable credibility.

Finally, the importance of securing national security goals should not be understated in the decision to form an MU (Willett 2000). The continuing tensions within the Middle East, which are unlikely to evaporate in the near future, demand a greater degree of political unity among the GCC states, which may indirectly be achieved through the goal of MU. A politically unified GCC would be more effective in acting as a 'countervailing influence against the domination of neighbouring powers', such as Iran and Iraq as well as giving the bloc greater confidence to push ahead with demands for a just and equitable solution to the Palestinian problem. According to Mundell (1997) such considerations could act as an important incentive for creating an MU. In fact, some analysts have attributed the formation of the GCC itself as a security reaction to the 1981 Iran–Iraq war and fears that Iran's Shia revolution might eventually be exported to them (Looney 2003). Kuwait in particular, will be keen to forge ahead with the economic and political integration process in order to strengthen its regional political alliances for the purposes of national security. Even though the economic case for Kuwait joining the MU is less pronounced than it is for other GCC states, it will not want to stay outside of the union in case the US decides to cut and run from Iraq leaving a security vacuum in that part of the region.

7 Prospects for GCC monetary union – a preliminary balance sheet

The key objective of this book has been to determine the appropriateness of MU for the GCC economic region. In order to achieve this, it firstly assessed the bloc against the OCA criteria (Chapter 3) and then measured the extent to which it has thus far met and is working towards meeting the European criteria (Chapter 4). Finally it focused on the potential costs and benefits of the MU project for the GCC (Chapters 5 and 6 respectively).

While we argue that there is an economic case for the GCC to forge ahead with its MU project, this book has shown that the progress made to date is insufficient. It points out that the necessary political determination and motivation needed to implement many of the European criteria are currently lacking. We also contend that institution building and fiscal and monetary convergence will have a greater bearing on the strength and sustainability of the common currency, than does the bloc's current standing vis-à-vis the OCA criteria.

The lack of progress towards MU is a consequence of several factors. The first being the oil price boom that started in 2002, as the huge windfall revenues seem to have reduced the imperative to carry out economic reforms, especially those at the regional level and those that involved the devolving of some sovereign powers. The second is that differences in inflation rates and economic development strategies have emerged in recent years. Some states may see advantages in a weak currency, while others do not; this means finding consensus on the format of a 'one size fits all' joint monetary policy may now be harder to achieve than previously envisaged, both by economists and ruling elites alike. The third factor is that the implicit need for fiscal restraint and greater budgetary transparency may be considered unpalatable by some ruling elites, and such requirements may not have been entirely apparent to the various parties when they first signed up to the project in 1981. Indeed such requirements only really became apparent during the EMU process in the 1990s.

In terms of the cost/benefit analysis, we argue that the *associated benefits*, arising from the process of forming an MU itself, are potentially as important, if not more so, than the conventional MU gains. The GCC will not benefit substantially from the elimination of exchange rate risk, as all but one of the prospective members have the same external exchange rate regime and therefore bilateral exchange rates are stable. It follows therefore, that the main cost of MU, the loss of independent monetary policy would also be small, as all have operated with a 'one size fits all' monetary policy, that of the US Federal Reserve for much of the period of analysis.

Nevertheless, from a dynamic perspective the weight of this cost may become more pronounced, many regional policymakers consider the current collective monetary policy to be unsuitable and there is now considerable inflation rate divergence. Theoretically, individual members could de-peg from the dollar today or revalue by different amounts deemed to be optimal for their own national economic circumstances. Such individual flexibility will not exist once tied together in MU. Going forward the cost of sharing the same monetary policy could become more significant than it is at present; especially if fiscal policy harmonization and the establishment of a common market does not take place. As we have alluded to previously, the debate over the utility of the dollar peg has intensified in recent years (see Chapter 8 for more on this).

Is the GCC an OCA (and does this matter?)

Our analysis shows that although the GCC meet some criteria they do not meet enough of them adequately to be considered an OCA. While failing to meet all of the OCA criteria might mean that MU is not 'optimal' for the GCC, as the Eurozone demonstrated, this does not make MU untenable or for that matter economically unbeneficial. Indeed the process of forming MU itself should lead to increasing levels of economic convergence, boost intra-regional trade intensity and deepen the region's capital markets.

Nevertheless, the OCA criteria remain a useful benchmark and political decisions (including commitment) may well be premised upon how well the region is perceived to shape up against them. Unlike Europe where a strong political motive supported the MU process, our analysis indicates that the GCC's MU project is to a larger extent underpinned and motivated by the assumed economic dividends. For this reason, the degree to which these states meet the OCA criteria will arguably have a greater bearing on the likelihood of MU coming into being than was the case for EMU. If GCC leaders do not feel the bloc scores well against these criteria, the political determination to forge ahead with the project may diminish, unless of course the associated benefits accruing from fulfilling the European criteria are given their due weight.

While it can be argued that the closer a given economic region is to meeting the criteria, the less costly MU will be, in the case of the GCC we consider other factors, many of which are part of the MU preparation process to more than compensate for any transitional and structural costs. This is why any MU cost/benefit analysis, especially in the context of the GCC, should not solely focus on the OCA criteria, but look at the associated economic benefits likely to arise from the preparation process itself. We will now summarize the findings of our OCA analysis.

Intra-regional trade

We do not consider the GCC to meet the trade criterion at present. It is clear that intra-GCC trade levels are low especially if compared to EMU's prior to 1999. This can largely be explained by the fact that all Gulf states export the same commodity; it follows that crude oil exporters are unlikely to want to import crude oil. Our analysis reveals however that if oil exports are factored out, intra-GCC trade triples and is actually larger than often assumed – from around five per cent of total exports to 16 per cent of non-crude oil exports. Using data for 1998 Jadresic (2002) factored out both crude oil and refined products and found that intra-GCC trade then represented more than a third of their total trade.

Our analysis of GCC trade intensity ratios also illustrates that intra-GCC trade is more pronounced than sometimes assumed. Trade levels between Bahrain and Saudi Arabia and between Oman and the UAE were both shown to be reasonably strong; both pairs of countries adjoin one another and have land border crossings. Furthermore, the findings of the GCC business survey indicate that intra-regional trade is particularly important for the Gulf's SMEs, which themselves form a large segment of the region's private sector.

In addition, trade is one criterion that is considered to be particularly endogenous – having an MU will in of itself lead to higher levels of trade. From a dynamic perspective (and irrespective of MU) we see several reasons for why intra-GCC trade in likely to increase in the foreseeable future. For example, Qatar has recently begun supplying natural gas to some of its Gulf neighbours, such as Oman and the UAE for their domestic electricity generation and as feed-stock in downstream heavy in industries; both Bahrain and Oman have only limited oil and gas reserves but are investing heavily in their respective refining, petrochemical and energy-heavy industrial sectors, therefore they will soon need to import greater volumes of oil and gas from their GCC neighbours. As all GCC states are now WTO members and investing in the diversification of their economies, setting up FTZs, building vast 'economic cities', establishing financial hubs, intra-regional trade opportunities should grow as a result.

Factor mobility

Turning to factor market mobility, we looked at two areas, labour and capital. With regard to labour we consider the GCC to meet this criterion satisfactorily, but in an unconventional way (relying on the elastic expatriate labour force). Nevertheless, some aspects of the GCC's present labour nationalization policies could erode the high levels of mobility which currently exist. Capital is also reasonably mobile within the bloc. There are no restrictions on capital flows and nationals (as well as foreign institutions) are able to invest in GCC-wide portfolio funds.

As with the more affluent citizens of the Eurozone, most GCC nationals are not geographically mobile, either between or within their respective states. Although GCC legislation has facilitated the cross-border movement and employment of nationals, few nationals opt to relocate for work purposes. The GCC meet the labour mobility criterion however because of the presence of a large, elastic pool of expatriate workers, comprising 62 per cent of their total labour force.

While most expatriates cannot move between the GCC states directly, they can do so by first returning to their home countries (from an economy that is perhaps contracting) and then re-migrating (to a neighbouring state whose economy is expanding). Since the start of the current oil price boom, wages in the private sector – where the majority of expatriates work – have not risen in line with inflation, demonstrating the shock absorptive capacity this cohort of labour clearly has. Such flexibility may be eroded however, if labour nationalization policies, replacing expatriates workers with nationals, are applied too rigidly to the private sector.

Turning to capital mobility, we consider the GCC meets this criterion reasonably well. The region's capital markets, especially since the start of the present oil price boom, are becoming more integrated. All GCC states now permit nationals from other member states to own and trade shares and Gulf citizens are increasingly willing to cross borders to invest in a neighbouring state's IPO. There is significant cross border cooperation on the issuance of Islamically compliant bonds and the intra-GCC debt market is likely to deepen considerably in the coming period. Finally, there is evidence that intra-GCC FDI has grown rapidly since the beginning of the decade.

Economic diversification

Although our findings show that the GCC states are not all that diversified, the fact that they are all undiversified in the *same manner* reduces somewhat the importance of this criterion. The GCC's shared oil dependence implies that all economies are likely to suffer from the same exogenous shock and, as such, it could be addressed with a single monetary policy. However, from a dynamic perspective evidence suggests that economic diversification throughout the GCC is taking place at differing speeds. As diversification occurs it is important that it takes place *within country* rather than simply *within region*. The idea that GCC countries should specialize in different industries to 'avoid competition' would result in the GCC economies becoming more vulnerable to asymmetric shocks.

Fortunately, given their similar comparative advantages there is evidence that the GCC are diversifying into similar areas. At least three capitals are vying for the position of being the Gulf's financial hub, many are now building up their tourism and hospitality sectors and airports and ports across the Gulf are being expanded and billed as key transport and trading hubs (several of these airports are being redesigned specifically to cater for the Airbus's new A380 and national carriers such as Emirates, Etihad and Qatar Airways together have placed the world's largest order for these new super-sized planes). All are investing in refineries and downstream petrochemical industries as well as industrial processes that are energy intensive.

Economic synchronization

The weight of evidence suggests that on the whole the region's economies follow a long-run cointegrating trend indicating that their business/economic cycles are quite well synchronized. The GCC economies remain dependent, albeit to varying degrees, on oil and therefore they tend to face the same external economic shock. However, some econometric analysis has found national disparities in terms of the degree of economic synchronization indicating that the response to these shocks may not be uniform, with Kuwait and the UAE appearing to be the most out of sync with other prospective members. In particular an analysis of the bilateral synchronization between the smaller states and the bloc's biggest economy, Saudi Arabia, reveals that synchronization between the two largest GCC economies – Saudi Arabia and the UAE– is weak. Consequently, a monetary policy predicated on the economic conditions of the more populous and economically dominant Saudi economy may not necessarily be optimal for the UAE or for that matter, for Kuwait.

Policy prerequisites for monetary union

Preparing for MU as opposed to inheriting one as a legacy of colonial rule involves a range of prerequisite policy reforms and institutional changes. As many of these policy prerequisites have become apparent during the EMU process we have referred to them as the *European criteria.* Despite setting out to emulate the process of EMU, it is clear that the GCC has made insufficient progress to date. In many ways it would appear that the GCC states fare better in terms of their structural suitability for MU vis-à-vis OCA criteria than they do in terms of their progress thus far in implementing the European criteria. It could be argued that not all these criteria are essential, but the weight of evidence suggests that without many of them an MU will a) be less beneficial and b) much harder to manage.

Several key hurdles remain including: completing the customs union; establishing a meaningful common market; and deciding upon the establishment and mandate of a GCC central bank. Others include improving the transparency and standardization of regional statistics, converging towards *appropriate* fiscal and monetary criteria and preparing the private sector. But, above all else, the political commitment to the very concept of MU and the determination to carry out sometimes difficult but necessary reforms, now seems to be less than wholehearted in the case of some GCC states.

As this book has shown individual GCC states do not seem willing to devolve sovereign power to pan-GCC institutions, as critically there has been no official agreement on the establishment of such institutions despite the substantial lead time required in their creation. If the GCC MU is to be anything more than a currency board, however, some form of centralized GCC central bank will need to be set up. Strong, autonomous institutions were pivotal to the successful launch of the euro, the GCC need to focus on these institutional issues in 2008–2009 otherwise the MU launch date is likely to end up being postponed.

Yet with regard to a GCC central bank several stumbling blocks are likely to emerge, and are probably already being fought over behind closed doors. These are: which country will host the institution and (far more importantly in our view) how will voting rights on future monetary policy decisions be allocated. If based on economic mass, Saudi Arabia would dominate yet such a situation is unlikely to be palatable to the other members; conversely, a one country one vote mechanism may be seen as giving disproportionate powers to the smaller economies.

The GCC finance ministers have agreed to adopt Maastricht-style convergence criteria yet rather than these being entrance *preconditions*, as they were in EMU, they appear to be *targets*, reducing the incentives for member states to meet them. The procyclical nature of GCC government budgets indicates that adhering to fiscal criteria over the medium to long run could prove to be particularly problematic. Furthermore, for effective monitoring of convergence and fiscal rules participating states will need to standardize their economic data and make this available to all other members on a timely basis. Post-MU this will also be essential in order to make informed decisions on the future monetary policy. Yet to date there has been no announcement regarding the creation of a pan-GCC statistical agency to create comparable data for the bloc and to produce data for the bloc as a whole.

The European criteria illustrate that, perhaps above all else, there needs to be a strong political desire and motive to enter into MU. While in the past GCC governments seem to have been motivated by the economic case and the success of EMU, a prolonged period of high oil prices beginning in 2002 seems to have reduced the imperative to forge ahead with deeper economic integration at the current juncture. For regional leaders to be sufficiently motivated to carry out such an ambitious project they will need to see not just economic dividends but also political-economy ones. It is our contention that if the associated benefits of MU are factored in, the GCC MU project can provide such dividends. MU is still clearly on the short-term agenda; the communiqué issued at the end of the 2007 GCC summit stating that GCC leaders remained committed to the MU and the launch date of 2010 (*Gulf News* 2007a).

Potential costs of GCC monetary union

This book has presented the first detailed assessment of the potential costs arising from the GCC MU project. Leaving aside for the moment the conventional cost of losing independent monetary policy, it contends that costs arising from the transition are essentially manageable and further that the magnitude of these will very much depend on the aforementioned political commitment to the process. Certain political-economy 'costs' – such as losing absolute sovereign control over fiscal policymaking, the need for greater economic disclosure and devolving some decision-making powers to supranational institutions may only be considered as costly for some ruling elites. Yet if economic reforms and policy prerequisites are not thorough in the lead-up to the launch date, the resultant MU may be harder to manage effectively and could prove to be more costly for the region.

Turning to the loss of monetary policy independence, just because all prospective members, with the exception of Kuwait, currently outsource their monetary policy to the US Federal Reserve, does not mean this is still considered to be an optimal arrangement. GCC leaders agreed to collectively stick with the dollar peg in the lead-up to MU, however, until a Gulf dinar is launched, any state could relatively easily relinquish the peg and regain control of independent interest rate setting, yet following MU this would no longer be an option. Therefore the loss of national autonomy over exchange rate policies inherent in MU could still prove costly for some states especially in light of diverging inflation rates, monetary policy preferences and economic development strategies.

Once tied into MU with countries experiencing lower inflation, higher inflation economies could experience further macroeconomic instability and competitive losses. The potential cost could indeed be significant given that inflation divergence among member states has been identified as a key reason for the disintegration of monetary unions (Nitsch 2005). Kuwait's May 2007 reversion back to its original trade-weighted basket peg and the GCC central bank governors' announcement in September 2007 that members will tackle their respective inflation rates independently is illustrative of the point that a unified external exchange rate policy under a future MU will not be cost free.

Even if the option to tackle national inflation rates independently in the lead-up to MU does not lead to greater monetary divergence, it demonstrates that reaching consensus on the choice of future monetary policy for the single currency will require substantial and ongoing compromises over the given states' national interests. Despite citing a lack of general progress on the path to MU Oman's exit from the project in our view is more likely to have stemmed from its preference for a weak currency in order to promote its non-oil export industries, a central theme of its economic development strategy, yet an exchange rate policy clearly at odds with those of other GCC states.

Despite agreeing to harmonize their economic policies in the 2001 Economic Agreement as part of the process towards full economic integration, to date these appear to be diverging, rather than converging, particularly in the fields of external trade, investment and labour nationalization policies. Post-MU policy divergence may be economically costly if it were to lead to greater macroeconomic divergence as this would be better dealt with by using a bespoke monetary policy. Yet, and despite all leaders signing up to the 2001 Economic Agreement, in the political context of the region, rulers are unused to compromising over their national economic policy decisions and doing so as part of the MU project will be considered as costly.

It is important that the monetary stability of the MU is not jeopardized by the fiscal indiscipline of a given member state therefore the GCC will need to agree upon a clear set of fiscal rules to follow and adhere to post-MU. However, we contend that the imposition of fiscal rules of the kind embodied in the Eurozone's SGP could be economically costly. The design of fiscal rules for the GCC must be tailored to the region's hydrocarbon dependency and their transitional stage of development otherwise they are unlikely to work in ensuring fiscal stability in the long run. In a political context we argue that the imposition of limits on fiscal spending and increased scrutiny of national public budgets that will necessarily need to take place – similar to the harmonization of macroeconomic policies above – may be considered as a diminution of their sovereignty.

The devolution of sovereign powers to supranational institutions will obviously entail costs at the national level in all states and probably explains why so little has been achieved in this respect to date. The issue is further complicated by the fact that the standards and integrity of existing national institutions will be pooled into supranational institutions meaning that those states with above GCC-average institutions may see a loss of institutional integrity. Without a strong mandate for the GCC central bank the location of the institution could become more important.

Finally, there are likely to be reservations among smaller states over entering into an MU with Saudi Arabia. Firstly, there is the concern that the Kingdom will use the project as a vehicle to exercise greater political influence over the Gulf. It may also steer the joint monetary decisions to suit the needs of its domestic economy at the expense of other member states. Secondly, the periphery states may be concerned that Saudi Arabia's image in the West of a somewhat politically and socially unstable regime will tarnish their reputations as 'safe havens' for FDI and international tourists. Conversely, Saudi Arabia may have some concerns of its own and may see deeper economic integration with its more liberal neighbours as politically costly, if such integration results in deepening the divide within Saudi society between those seeking greater personal freedoms and those that feel the Kingdom has already gone too far in this regard.

Potential benefits of GCC monetary union

Based on the assumption that the necessary preparatory steps are taken, the economic case for forming an MU is favourable, as we have said many associated benefits are likely to arise from the process of preparing for MU itself. It should be noted nevertheless that most existing research on the GCC MU project predicts only limited benefits. This is primarily because historically intra-GCC exchange rates have been relatively stable and the trade-related gains are often deemed to be minimal. This summary will first look at the *direct benefits* and then consider the *associated benefits*.

According to economic theory the direct microeconomic benefits arising from forming an MU stem from the transaction cost savings and the removal of exchange rate risk on intra-regional trade and investment. While these gains may indeed be small for the GCC, the longer term potential for a common market and single currency to increase future trade intensity between the GCC states is not. The findings of a GCC business survey also indicate that such savings may be particularly significant for SMEs which form a large share of the private sector and for whom the burden of currency-related transaction costs weighs heavier than for larger companies.

Other efficiency gains will be contingent upon whether a common market is first in place. For example the launch of the single currency will allow for greater price transparency between GCC markets, but consumers will only benefit from reduced price discrimination and price convergence if there is increased goods market arbitrage by way of a more complete common market. However, evidence from a regional business survey indicates that price differences across the GCC may persist as a result of other transaction costs such as differences in local taxes, fees, overhead and distribution costs. Thus in tandem with establishing a common market supplementary reforms aimed at harmonizing business regulations would ideally also take place. The planned GCC-wide railway network should reduce distribution costs somewhat.

The creation of an enlarged single market can be expected to provide benefits for the smaller GCC economies allowing them to take advantage of greater economies of scale in production through access to a much larger market of potential customers. At the same time, the effect will be to increase intra-GCC competition, which should also be beneficial for all member states by improving efficiencies, strengthening businesses and generating welfare gains for consumers. GCC business survey findings indicate that, on the whole, businesses are supportive of the MU project and therefore the effect of the single currency on private sector confidence and the business climate is likely to be positive. The private sector is also confident about the potential impact of MU on their businesses which bodes well for future investment decisions and potential economic growth both in the lead-up to and post-MU.

One area which this book has identified as a key beneficiary of a future MU is the Gulf's capital markets. Reduced cross-border risks will improve the mechanisms for an efficient allocation of capital across the region which should reduce the cost of capital for the private sector. The benefits for the region's capital markets are therefore important for private sector investment and growth and thus the broader economic development and diversification of the region. The region's fast growing Islamic financial services market is also likely to deepen once a single currency is launched aiding the GCC's goal of becoming the global hub for Islamic finance.

A key *associated benefit* of GCC MU is, in our view, that the MU process could act as a catalyst for undertaking economic reforms in the region. Once member states are tied together in MU, the need for transparent and standardized budget reporting will be vital as all members will face the economic repercussions of any one government's unsustainable spending and borrowing. Improvements in data transparency and fiscal accountability will not only lead to more balanced and sustainable growth but are also likely to make the region much more attractive to international investors. While we have acknowledged that such implicit pressures for greater transparency may be viewed as politically 'costly' by some groups in the long run such reforms will undoubtedly prove to be beneficial for GCC economic diversification and development. For those members striving to break away from dependence on hydrocarbons and the trappings of rentierism, the MU project will be seen as the ideal vehicle to drive through with such reforms.

Another associated benefit of MU will be to strengthen the bloc as a cohesive integrated entity. Post-MU the GCC states will have a much stronger voice with regard to international disputes and negotiations. Sharing a common currency should also expand their sphere of influence on the global financial stage. The common exchange rate policy and movement of a Gulf dinar – bearing in mind their hydrocarbon endowments and huge financial surpluses – will be closely watched from Tokyo through to London and New York. A unified regional bloc acting with one voice will also give the views of the GCC states greater political weight when seeking to influence US and EU foreign policy on the Middle East. In addition there are also potential geopolitical and financial rewards if the future Gulf dinar were to become a more independent currency; these are discussed in Chapter 8.

Will all GCC states be winners?

Although the following preliminary assessment of whether each Gulf state stands to gain from joining the MU is not comprehensive, it does nevertheless provide some indication as to which members have the most, or least, to gain from the MU project. This first assessment is based mainly on the contemporary economic and political circumstances of the GCC states. However, we must stress that post-2010 depending on the extent of convergence/divergence the distribution of these benefits across the bloc could change. Furthermore, as we shall see in Chapter 8 the overall gains to the GCC will also be partly contingent on what sort of MU the GCC leaders adopt and what they decide to do with the Gulf dinar – stick with the peg and keep it a passive currency or opt for an alternative regime and possibly allow it to float and become an independent currency.

Relatively speaking, the net economic benefits of MU are likely to be greatest for Bahrain and the UAE. Not only are these economies extremely open with strong existing intra-regional trade links, but they are also relatively well diversified and have existing comparative advantages in many service sector activities including banking, finance and tourism – areas which, as we established, should do particularly well from the launch of the single currency. However, the UAE is by far the most dynamic and liberal of the GCC economies and it may therefore have the greatest concerns over the potential cost of joining an MU with the much more conservative Saudi Arabia. Signals from the UAE are nevertheless mixed the Central Bank Governor, Sultan Al-Suwaidi, has been very vocal in stressing the importance of the GCC taking collective monetary policy decisions in the short term so as to ensure that they continue to be unified in the lead-up to MU. Yet Al-Suwaidi has been the only GCC central bank governor thus far to suggest that the launch date may need to be postponed.

Compared to the other GCC states, Kuwait and Qatar stand to gain less in economic terms. Both presently have limited trade with other GCC states and Kuwait seems quite happy pursuing its own independent monetary policy. Due to their vast per capita hydrocarbon reserves neither state faces a serious imperative to diversify for at least several generations indicating that they may be less willing to make compromises in favour of common goals. However, this does not mean that there are not other incentives to join. Qatar's ambitions of building a trans-Gulf natural gas pipeline with which to supply the domestic energy needs of many of its GCC neighbours would be facilitated by its inclusion in the MU. For Kuwait, further integration with its Gulf neighbours, particularly with Saudi Arabia, is likely to be considered important for its national security in light of ongoing instability in Iraq. Despite it having a different monetary arrangement than the other four prospective members, it still officially intends to become a member and views its current monetary policy divergence as a short-term necessity.

There is a strong case for Saudi Arabia to join the MU. Businesses based in the Kingdom, particularly those in the petrochemicals and heavy industries sectors are well placed to enter other GCC markets and their existing economies of scale should provide them with competitive advantages. Saudi Arabia is a major beneficiary of GCC direct investment and this is expected to increase following MU, as currency transaction costs are eliminated and a single Gulf dinar allows for better price comparisons. There may also be political gains from its membership. As we have noted earlier, it may be able to exercise greater leverage over its smaller neighbours and possibly become the leading voice of the GCC bloc on the international stage.

While Saudi Arabia's economic mass and large domestic market offer the other states many opportunities and the Gulf dinar would become a far more significant and globally recognized currency with the Kingdom on board, as we have previously alluded to concerns over Saudi dominance and its slow pace of economic reform are no doubt considered as associated MU costs by some of its more dynamic neighbours. While MU without Saudi Arabia would mean the Gulf dinar would be a less high-profile currency, it could still be a viable monetary option for the smaller more economically liberal states. By the same token, given the fact that both the GCC Secretariat and the Monetary Union Unit are based in Riyadh, if Saudi Arabia were to opt out, it could be, in our view, a death blow to the whole project.

Although the evidence presented in this book suggests that all GCC states can expect to accrue net economic benefits from entering into an MU, it is impossible for us to gauge just how much of a compromise greater budgetary disclosure and fiscal accountability will be viewed by each individual member state. These 'costs' along with each member's willingness to devolve a degree of national decision-making power to supranational institutions will ultimately, in our view, be the key factors in a given member state's decision on whether or not to join the MU.

8 Future issues and controversies

Much of the following analysis is necessarily speculative but the issues discussed are fundamental in determining whether the GCC MU project will progress from the drawing board and, if so, in what particular manner a future Gulf dinar will interface with the wider economic and political world. In our view, two issues need addressing, firstly, what shape and form will the Gulf dinar take. By considering post-2010 external exchange rate regimes today, GCC policymakers should be able to minimize the inherent problems associated with a 'one size fits all' monetary policy. Secondly, what, if any, are the geopolitical implications? Will the Gulf dinar be seen as an Islamic and Middle Eastern anchor currency? Is it conceivable that it may one day be used to invoice some of the Gulf's oil sales? Undoubtedly, the Gulf's central bankers will be evaluating similar questions and their conclusions may well tip the balance on whether or not to proceed.

We will start, however, by briefly returning to the question of whether the bloc's considerable dependence on income from oil and gas *in and of itself* reduces the probability of the MU project actually becoming a reality. To what extent will these 'rentier state' characteristics constitute an obstacle to the likelihood of a GCC MU if at all? On the one hand, it could be argued that because of the Gulf's resource wealth it has the financial means to easily implement the project. Combined with the respective governments' clear willingness to mobilize a significant portion of their revenues for social and welfare investments, they should not therefore face the sort of widespread public distrust and dissent which accompanied the moves towards MU in Europe and which resulted in the UK, Sweden and Denmark remaining outside of the Eurozone. In the interviews with regional experts, only one of 40 (an academic from Oman) thought that national attachment to existing sovereign currencies might be an issue. On the other hand, the entrenched patronage systems and 'off-balance sheet' behaviour – often present in 'rentier state' economies – will, as part of the MU process, necessarily come under more scrutiny. Greater budgetary disclosure and transparency are essential for the smooth operating of a joint currency and therefore such factors may act as a powerful disincentive.

Nevertheless, when discussing this issue in Chapter 2 we saw no compelling reason for why such traits should impede or derail the process. Gabon, a member of the French franc zone, exhibits many similar attributes (Zafar 2004) and, like the GCC states, derives most of its external rent from the same commodity. Yet despite suffering from periods of 'Dutch disease' and sharing a joint currency with a group of members, many of who do not have hydrocarbon endowments, membership of an MU has not adversely affected Gabon's economic performance. Indeed, it is argued that Gabon's MU membership has contributed to low inflation and prevented it from 'monetizing its deficits through printing of money' (Zafar 2004: 9–10).

What sort of currency?

It would be prudent for the GCC to decide in advance what sort of monetary regime the new currency will adopt both for the transitional process and post-MU. The debate will no doubt focus on whether to continue to outsource monetary policy to the US or to assume greater control over monetary policy by moving to a more flexible exchange rate arrangement. In 2006 the UAE central bank governor, Sultan Al-Suwaidi, suggested that de-pegging from the dollar would take place at some point after 2010 saying that the single currency 'will be for a bigger geographical area that will have a bigger weight on the international arena, so it will have to be floated then' (Khalaf 2006).

Some other central bankers might not be so brave, and may consider that a free floating Gulf dinar would be too susceptible to speculative attacks and volatility. Most would, however, consider a greater degree of flexibility than exists at present as an advantage, as this would help the bloc to adjust more rapidly to oil price movements. A trade-weighted basket peg that stabilizes the real exchange rate and helps maintain the competitiveness of the non-oil-dependent export sector is a distinct possibility. The GCC could even decide to align the Gulf dinar to the prevailing price of oil – possibly by factoring the price of oil into the trade-weighted basket equation.

Equally though, fearing US disquiet over the abandonment of the dollar, they may simply opt to maintain the status quo, albeit with the odd collective revaluation. At the time of writing, however, the dollar's continued decline against other major trading currencies was leading to considerable speculation that the Gulf's present exchange rate regime may need altering prior to 2010 and the 'benefits' of the status quo were becoming harder to discern.

Maintaining the dollar peg

Advocates of the status quo argue that the region's dollar peg has assisted in facilitating a low inflationary environment for much of the bloc's history and given GCC monetary policy substantial credibility. The main economic case for pegging to the dollar has been based on the fact that as GCC oil exports are denominated in dollars and therefore pegging matches the currency of the GCC's 'assets' with its 'liabilities' or domestic spending commitments. Also by pegging to the currency of an oil importer the GCC economies have, to a certain extent, avoided the problems associated with a rapidly appreciating currency, yet as our analysis has shown the GCC have still been prone to bouts of 'Dutch disease'.

While the nominal exchange rate may remain stable during times of high oil prices, it often leads to an appreciation of real exchange rates, which in turn can adversely affect the competitiveness of non-oil exports. On the import side of the GCC's trade balance sheet a large share of Asian imports are still invoiced in dollars (although this is changing) and therefore, until recently, the dollar peg has also limited the risk on import costs.

Although outsourcing monetary policy in their early stages of economic development may have been beneficial to the region, as the GCC economies have matured it has become increasingly apparent that the adoption of a more flexible exchange rate regime with greater interest rate setting independence would be more beneficial. Pegging to the dollar has meant that GCC central banks have not been able to actively use independent monetary policy tools which has led to much larger economic swings reflected in the volatility of GCC GDP since 1980 (see Table 2.3). During periods of low oil prices economic growth stagnated and could not be stimulated by an expansionary monetary policy, conversely, during periods of high oil prices they have not been able to increase interest rates to combat inflation.

Despite stabilizing GCC export revenues, pegging to the dollar also leaves the GCC exposed to considerable exchange rate risk on the import side of their trade balance. Its imports are increasingly sourced from non-dollar countries, only 11 per cent of total imports were from the US in 2006. Thus the dollar's depreciation against the euro and the yen means that the GCC has lost substantial purchasing power. Imports from the EU and non-dollar Asian countries accounted for 48 per cent of GCC total imports (the share of total GCC imports from the EU in 2006 constituted the largest share of total GCC imports at 29 per cent). Five of the most significant Asian exporters to the GCC in 2006 – including India, Japan and South Korea – are not pegged to the dollar, although we acknowledge that they may use the dollar as a vehicle currency for trade. As many Gulf states, especially the UAE, import large volumes of Toyotas from Japan, it would make economic sense for them to invoice some of their oil and gas sales to Japan in yen.

As a consequence of the dollar peg and 'petrodollar recycling', until recently much of the region's offshore assets have been dollar denominated and, therefore, it is often assumed that they have a vested interest in maintaining the peg, as a move away from it would cause the dollar and concomitantly their assets to lose value. Furthermore, it is often contended that as the majority of GCC assets have been held in dollars, it is prudent to continue with the dollar peg for the time being (Abed *et al.* 2003). Yet there is now some preliminary evidence that GCC central banks are increasingly opting to hold their reserves in stronger currencies such as the euro (Bank for International Settlements 2005). Furthermore the bloc's sovereign wealth funds are increasingly looking at higher yield investments (much of these funds are flowing East and range from building commercial and residential neighbourhoods in Bangalore and Mumbai to stakes in Chinese banks).

With signs that high oil prices are here to stay, without a nominal exchange rate appreciation the Gulf states are likely to suffer from higher inflation rates and real exchange rates for some time to come. These states could, of course, stick with the dollar peg but revalue the rate at which they fix their currencies; an appreciation of as much as 15 to 20 per cent has been suggested. And while those states seeking to expand their non-oil export industries, may view this as too large a revaluation, they may be failing to recognize that they are still facing a loss of competitiveness through an appreciation of their real exchange rates. In addition a revaluation may only bring temporary respite as it itself may force the dollar to devalue further and they would again find themselves in essentially the same position.

In our view, being tied to US interest rates can now *only be considered* as a sub-optimal policy choice for the GCC. Monetary policy set by the US Federal Reserve is tailored for the needs of the US economy – a major oil importer not those of the oil-exporting GCC states. Oil price shocks in the US are more often dealt with through monetary policy loosening which often leads to more inflationary pressure in the Gulf economies. Since 2002 rising oil prices have coincided with very low US interest rates which fell to one per cent in 2003 and although, for a while, they rose from very low levels loosening began again in mid-2007, causing real GCC interest rates to turn negative. All this helped fuel the GCC stock markets to unsustainable levels in 2005 (see Figure 3.4) and is continuing to fuel the unprecedented asset price boom.

Alternative regimes

There are potentially significant direct and indirect economic benefits to be gained from moving to a more flexible exchange rate arrangement. Critically, it would allow the GCC states to operate an independent monetary policy predicated on the region's economic circumstances and not those of the domestic US economy with which they are increasingly out of sync. A more flexible option would help to stabilize import costs rather than just export revenues and protect the purchasing power of the region's increasingly diversified assets; it may also help bolster efforts at economic diversification through improving exchange rate competitiveness.

While the choice of exchange rate policy post-MU remains uncertain, increasingly it appears as though the dollar peg had outlived its usefulness. Most regional experts interviewed by the author felt that a more flexible exchange rate regime would be preferable as it would allow the bloc to adjust to global economic shocks and move interest rates in response to regional economic conditions. There is also evidence to suggest that commodity exporters would have greater exchange rate stability from a free floating exchange rate regime over a peg to the dollar (Setser 2007).

Assuming the GCC states successfully launch a single currency there are several potential exchange rate regime options open to them. Leaving aside the *status quo*, the three main options being considered are a free float, a continued peg but to a mixed basket or possibly-trade-weighted basket of currencies and the possibility of linking the future currency in some way to the price of oil. While a free float could provide greater flexibility and competitiveness than would opting to peg to a trade-weighted basket of currencies, the latter is more likely in the years immediately post MU, Kuwait already has a similar mechanism and thus can provide guidance (its central bank has managed a basket peg for many years without any known difficulties).

The free float and trade-weighted exchange rate regime options also entail potential costs. On the cost side, a peg to a basket of currencies may be less transparent and more difficult for GCC institutions to manage. Some expert interviewees felt that a free floating Gulf dinar may be too volatile and the subject of repeated speculative attacks. Yet the GCC's ample foreign reserves would provide a cushion against any speculative attacks and initially a managed float within a reference band could be opted for which would provide a greater degree of stability but at the same time allowing for exchange rate adjustments. Of course it will only be possible to manage a free floating or a trade-weighted basket if there were a strong and credible GCC central bank in place. If a GCC central bank with adequate decision-making powers and institutional capabilities is not established, then the dollar peg is likely to remain in place.

Some economists have argued that pegging to the price of oil makes sense for commodity exporters (Frankel 2003) in that the value of the domestic currency will fluctuate in line with oil prices which could ease the adjustment to oil price shocks. Thus as the oil price rises the currency would appreciate and purchasing power would strengthen, conversely as oil prices fell the currency would depreciate making non-oil exports cheaper. Indeed, a free floating Gulf dinar would likely be characterized as a 'commodity currency' as its value would reflect the price of oil and rise and fall in line with it. Moreover, the GCC states may choose to invoice their oil sales in the new currency, requesting payment in Gulf dinars in their long-term oil contracts. They could even sell shorter term contracts on one of the region's energy bourses (rather than on international markets) and allow the buyer to decide which currency to pay in – dollars, euros, Gulf dinars or yen.

Such a switch would create additional demand for the nascent currency as central banks in other countries would want to hold Gulf dinars in their reserves in order to cover the costs of their oil purchases. One advantage of this outcome would be that an increased overseas demand for the Gulf dinar would provide the bloc with seigniorage revenues – a welcome non-oil income for the region. It would also strengthen the currency and should make it an attractive anchorage currency for other countries to peg their exchange rates against. Contrariwise, such an arrangement could be problematic for GCC export diversification, as non-oil exports would become less competitive if the new currency were to appreciate too much. In addition, fluctuations in oil prices may lead to exchange rate volatility and it has been suggested that a more appropriate option might be – as alluded to previously – to stick with some form of peg to a basket of currencies but include in it the price of oil.

One thing is clear, the choice of exchange rate regime for the Gulf dinar will not be an easy one. Much will depend on the prevailing economic conditions in the coming years and will require member states to make some compromises. If, post-MU, disagreements about the appropriate alternative to the dollar peg persist, it is likely that the current exchange rate regime will be kept as a compromise solution.

Geopolitical implications

Despite the strong economic case for the GCC to abandon the dollar peg and switch to a more flexible and independent arrangement there may be political and security factors which prevent them from doing so. Such a move may not be well received by the US – the main arms supplier and source of security for the GCC states. Referring to Saudi Arabia, Robinson and Morse (2007) argue that the Kingdom has thus far been reluctant to do anything that would jeopardize its political alliance with the US. We argue that while at this present conjuncture the US Federal Reserve may see the weakening dollar as advantageous; the US administration would not welcome a Saudi (or GCC-wide) move to de-peg from the dollar – it could start a chain reaction of selling dollars. Nevertheless, there are a number of longer term strategic and geopolitical considerations implicit in the establishment of an *independent* single currency which may provide an overriding incentive for the GCC states to move to a flexible exchange rate regime.

Should the GCC leaders opt for an independent exchange rate regime and monetary policy then the GCC currency may become something of a regional currency and could used as an anchorage and reserve currency for neighbouring Middle Eastern and Islamic states. Depending on the strength and stability of the Gulf dinar, other Muslim and Arab countries might choose to peg their currencies to it and those countries with strong trade links to the region might also choose to hold it in their foreign reserves. Furthermore, if the GCC leaders chose to invoice (some or all of) their oil sales in the new currency this would generate increased demand for it and generate substantial seigniorage revenues. As well as the financial gains for the GCC states, the emergence of the Gulf dinar as a regional currency would, perhaps more importantly, give the GCC states substantial prestige across the Arab and Islamic world.

Our interviews with GCC experts revealed that they were equally split on the prospect of the Gulf dinar becoming a regional reserve and anchorage currency. It was felt that it would be contingent on a range of economic and political factors. These included the development and diversification of these economies and the degree to which transparency and accountability were improved. Also it was argued that to a certain extent it would also depend on the performance and mandate of the future GCC central bank. While many experts interviewed felt that the GCC, as an economic region, would be too insignificant for its future common currency to become an anchorage and reserve currency, several did see some potential. One government official in the UAE felt that:

> It is conceivable, for example investors hold Swiss francs in reserves. If you achieve a reputation for low inflation and stability and you have good policies it may be attractive for neighbouring countries, such as Iran and Pakistan, whom you trade with to hold your currency in reserve.

Another expert, this time a Qatari Central Bank official said: 'The huge oil and gas reserves of the GCC states along with large financial reserves and current account surpluses are factors that will influence the single currency's ability to become a reserve currency'. In the current political climate, one consideration could become extremely influential in determining the GCC's choice of exchange rate and monetary policy. The Gulf dinar, if successful, could be perceived as an alternative *Islamic currency*, providing a religious motivation for holding the currency in addition to the economic rationale outlined above. Although the GCC single currency would not technically be Islamic (monetary policy is considered to be contrary to Sharia law), all GCC states are Islamic and there is a wide range of Islamically compliant investment opportunities within the region, some of which will no doubt be denominated in Gulf dinars post-2010. The central banks of Islamic countries such as Indonesia, Malaysia and Pakistan may be inclined to hold what they perceive to be a more 'acceptable' currency in their reserves in light of the general sentiment in the Islamic world that holding currency reserves in dollars has helped fund some of the current US administration's controversial policies in the Middle East.

With regard to invoicing future GCC oil sales in Gulf dinars several interviewees felt that there would be economic benefits but the majority considered the potential political cost of such a move would be too high. For this reason, most felt that the likelihood of the GCC states invoicing oil in their new single currency was unlikely in the short to medium term. An independent research analyst in the UAE said: 'Such a move would provoke hostility from the US and would be politically risky. The margin of economic benefit does not outweigh the political risk.'

However, this would not exclude the possibility of invoicing a proportion of oil sales in the new currency. It is known that Iran is paid in yen for some of its hydrocarbon exports to Japan and also that Russia receives some payments in euros for the gas it sells to Europe. As opposed to arbitrarily ditching the dollar – which would undoubtedly cause some disquiet in Washington – the GCC could post-2010 accept payments in a range of currencies including its own, this could not be construed as a political move but rather a 'free market' one.

The immediate outlook

As all participating Arabian Peninsula states are geographically contiguous, have a common language and culture, not just as Arabs but more specifically as *Khaleeji* (Gulf Arabs), the GCC should not face the same problems that policy-makers in EMU did when trying to convince a sceptical public that the euro would not erode cultures or lead to the loss of national identities. Yet, as this book goes to press, it remains far from certain whether a Gulf dinar will come into being, as per schedule in 2010.

Several questions remain: Does such ambiguity at this late stage indicate that the bloc is not actually all that suitable for MU or that the preparation process is proving to be more difficult to achieve than originally thought or that the prerequisite political commitment is lacking? For answers it is once more worth turning to the EMU experience for guidance.

Prior to the euro, EMU economies, much like those of the Gulf today, were not considered to represent a perfect OCA. Not constituting an OCA however, did not prevent 11 European countries forging ahead with their MU plans. It follows that this fact alone is unlikely to derail the GCC MU. Indeed, the introduction of the euro has generally been regarded as a success story. The ECB is a widely respected independent institution, the Eurozone's capital markets have deepened and most telling the euro is now rivalling the dollar as the world's reserve currency of choice.

It is true that the GCC's fiscal and monetary convergence process has been marginal at best; firstly, it is not clear what steps, if any, are being taken towards meeting them. It is also unclear what effective means, if any, will be available for enforcing them. Secondly, they seem to have been for the most part copied from those in the EMU's Maastricht criteria. This book has argued that this may be inappropriate and although the GCC Monetary Union Unit have tailored them somewhat to suit the region's economic idiosyncrasies, they are likely to need adjusting further. EMU had problems with the SGP and subsequently was forced to modify the fiscal rules. Furthermore, the areas of monetary convergence in which the Gulf had been excelling– stable bilateral exchange rates and interest rates – may now possibly be subject to more divergence.

However, some MU specialists argue that monetary convergence targets are not as important as is institution building and others consider them to be partly endogenous. We contend that to measure and monitor convergence a pan-GCC statistical institution should be created. Yet, and critically, there is still time for a greater degree of convergence to take place if the political will and determination is strong during 2008 and 2009. Convergence in EMU only really occurred in the final stages and was largely a result of political will.

The principal lesson the EMU experience provides any economic region considering MU is that a strong level of political motivation is absolutely essential and furthermore that supranational institutions (and the process of institution building) are integral to the success of MU. In terms of timeframes, full economic integration in the Eurozone took close to 50 years to achieve (starting with the creation of the European Payments Union). The GCC only came into being in 1981.

It is our contention that if the necessary policy prerequisites, especially the institutional ones, are not fully in place prior to 2010, two outcomes are likely. The first and most probable will be the deferral of the project (possibly to 2015), while the second would be a loosely managed joint currency incapable of moving away from the dollar peg, or some form of currency board, which would also limit the choice of external exchange rate regime options.

While we consider any transition that enables the GCC to regain more control over its monetary policy (particularly the ability to set interest rates best suited to the Gulf's prevailing economic conditions) to be advantageous, for the bloc to accrue many of the *associated benefits* this book has indicated the GCC MU project could provide, a considerable amount of work needs to be done between now and 2010. The costs associated with putting the region's longer term interests ahead of the short-term national ones are not insignificant, neither will be the level of political determination required to make the region's budgetary processes more transparent and standardized. We consider, however, that these are costs well worth bearing for the longer term benefits of greater economic diversification and more balanced and sustainable economic growth which the MU project can provide.

Notes

1 Introduction

1 The ECCU comprises Antigua and Barbuda, Grenada, Saint Kitts and Nevis, Dominica, Saint Lucia, Saint Vincent and the Grenadines and two British-controlled territories of Anguilla and Montserrat. The East Caribbean dollar has been pegged at a fixed exchange rate to the US dollar since July 1976 at EC$2.70 to US$1.

2 There are three French franc MU zones. The first, Communauté Financière Africaine, comprises Benin, Burkina Faso, Côte d'Ivoire, Guinea-Bissau, Mali, Niger, Sénégal and Togo; the second, Coopération Financière en Afrique Central, comprises Cameroon, Central African Republic, Chad, Republic of the Congo, Equatorial Guinea, Gabon; and the third zone, the Comptoirs Français du Pacifique, comprises New Caledonia, French Polynesia and the Wallis and Futuna Islands. As of January 2002 the fixed-peg exchange rates were CFA 655.957 to €1 and CFP 119.253 to €1.

3 This was also known as the Persian Gulf rupee and the External Indian rupee. It was issued by the Reserve Bank of India and was pegged to the Indian rupee which itself was pegged to the British pound.

4 A GCC Business Survey along with interviews with regional experts was carried out by the author in 2005. The GCC Business Survey received 307 responses from businesses across the six GCC states and interviews with 40 experts, including central bank governors, policymakers, academics and commercial bankers, were conducted in various GCC capitals. For more details see Rutledge (2007, 2008).

2 Characteristics of the GCC economies

1 The Standard Drawing Right is an international reserve asset created by the IMF and officially defined as a basket of currencies consisting of the euro, Japanese yen, pound sterling and US dollar. The weights in the basket are currently EUR 34%, JPY 11%, GBP 11%, USD 44%.

2 The REER is obtained by adjusting the NEER for inflation differentials with the countries whose currencies are included in the basket. The NEER is a weighted average of major bilateral nominal exchange rates, with weights based on the trade shares reflecting the relative importance of each currency in the effective exchange rate basket.

3 Figures calculated from OPEC Annual Statistical Bulletins, various issues.

3 Is the GCC an optimal currency area?

1 According to Jadresic (2002) intra-GCC exports stood at 34.1 per cent of total non-crude oil and non-crude oil product exports in 1998. Due to data limitations it was not possible to calculate this ratio for a more recent year.

2 The TIR is calculated as: $T_{ij} = (x_{ij}/X_{it})/(x_{wj}/X_{wt})$ Where x_{ij} and x_{wj} are the values of

country i's exports and of world exports to country j and where Xit and Xwt are country i's total exports and total world exports respectively.

3 Bahrain is an island. The King Fahd Causeway was built between Bahrain and Saudi Arabia in 1986.

4 There is no common definition for SMEs in the Gulf or the wider Middle East for that matter. As a reference point, SMEs in Europe are defined as businesses with up to 250 employees and an annual turnover of less than €50 million.

5 According to one estimate, small businesses in Saudi Arabia represent almost 93 per cent of total enterprises and account for about 25 per cent of total employment (Sajini 2004).

6 The institution won EuroMoney's award for best domestic market *sukuk* house in 2005.

7 In addition, two UAE banks have branches in Bahrain, Oman and Qatar. One Omani bank has a branch in the UAE and has bought an existing bank in Bahrain (Fasano and Staff Team 2003).

8 Figures calculated from AMF (2006 and various issues).

9 For example, the issue of regional competition was considered to be of such importance that it was the topic of a Bahrain Economic Society conference, entitled 'GCC 2010: From Competition to Integration', held in Bahrain on 23–24 November 2004. In addition, a number of regional experts interviewed by the author for this research also felt that increasing intra-regional competition might be detrimental to the region's integration efforts.

4 Policy prerequisites for GCC monetary union

1 Part of the material presented in this chapter is based on Rutledge (2008a).

2 Saudi Arabia for example is the only GCC state which issues debt instruments with a maturity of ten years.

5 Potential costs of GCC monetary union

1 In its 2005 Article Four, Consultation with the UAE, the IMF said that it needed to adopt a consistent and comprehensive set of public sector fiscal accounts, 'consolidated fiscal accounts for the seven Emirates and the Federal government based on harmonized classifications and methodologies will need to be developed and be available without significant delay' (IMF 2005a).

2 Such as the dispute between the UAE and Saudi Arabia over the waters of Al-Adeed. In the mid-1970s the UAE ceded a small piece of land to Saudi Arabia in a border agreement but retained sovereign rights over the waters; Saudi Arabia still disputes this.

6 Potential benefits of GCC monetary union

1 When the 95 per cent confidence interval for this proportion was calculated, the confidence limits – between 80% and 88% – confirmed that a comfortable majority of businesses held this view.

2 For example in November 2007 the UAE dirham surged to a 17-year high against the dollar and some other Gulf currencies as speculators bet on an appreciation of the dirham.

3 The upper and lower bounds of the 95 per cent confidence interval for this 76 per cent 'optimistic' reply was calculated at between 71% and 81%.

4 The upper and lower bounds of the 95 per cent confidence interval for this reply were again calculated at between 71% and 81%.

Bibliography

Aarts, P. (1999) 'The Middle East: a region without regionalism or the end of exceptionalism?', *Third World Quarterly*, Journal of Emerging Areas, Vol. 20, No. 5: 911–925.

Abdul Ghafour, P.K. (2006) 'Aramco, total sign deal for $6bn refinery', *Arab News*, 22 May.

—— (2005) 'Saudi Arabia gives equal treatment for share trading', *Arab News*, 5 April.

Abed, G.T., Erbas, S.N. and Guerami, B. (2003) 'The GCC monetary union: some considerations for the exchange rate regime', *IMF Working Paper*, Washington, DC: International Monetary Fund, April.

Aburish, S. (1995) *The Rise, Corruption and Coming Fall of the House of Saud*, London: Bloomsbury Publishing.

Ahmad, M. (2005) 'Stock mania adds to delays in government office', *Arab News*, 11 May.

Al-Hajji, A.F. (1999) 'A special interview with Robert Mundell – nobel laureate in economics', *Al Watan*, December.

Al-Hakeem, M. (2006) 'GCC to require price tags in all Gulf currencies', *Gulf News*, 10 July.

Al-Hassan, A., Delgado, F. and Omran, M. (2007) 'IPO behavior in GCC countries: goody-two shoes or bad-to-the-bone?', *IMF Working Paper WP/07/149*, Washington, DC: International Monetary Fund, Middle East and Central Asia Department, July.

Al-Mansouri, A.K.L. and Dziobek, C. (2006) 'Providing official statistics for the common market and monetary union in the Gulf Cooperation Council (GCC) Countries – a case for "Gulfstat"', *IMF Working Paper WP/06/38*, Washington, DC: International Monetary Fund, February.

Al-Sadik, A.T. (2006) 'GCC stock market developments in 2005', *Gulf Yearbook 2005–2006*, Dubai: Gulf Research Center.

Al-Saud, A.A (2002) 'Address to the Gulf Cooperation Council', *Middle East Policy*, Vol. IX, No. 1, March.

Al-Qudsi, S.S. (2006) 'Unemployment evolution in the GCC economies: its nature and relationship to output gaps', *Labour Market Studies*, Center for Market Research & Information, June.

Al-Uwaisheg, A.H. (2003) 'Search for criteria of economic convergence in the GCC area', paper presented at the European Commission Conference, *Europe, the Mediterranean and the Euro*, Athens, Greece, 3 February.

Ameen, A. (2006a) 'GCC to introduce common currency on time in 2010', *Gulf News*, 9 October.

—— (2006b) 'GCC Central Bank to be located in Abu Dhabi', *Gulf News*, 19 September.

AMEInfo (2006a) 'Regional project values top $1 trillion', 22 April. Available at www.ameinfo.com/83678.html (accessed 12 November 2006).

—— (2006b) 'Six HyperPandas for UAE', 12 April. Available at www.ameinfo.com/82832.html (accessed 28 June 2006).

—— (2005) 'UAQ, $8.2bn Tameer city project', 26 July. Available at www.ameinfo.com/64854.html (accessed 12 November 2005).

AMF (2007) *Databank for Arab Stock Markets*, Quarterly Bulletin, Quarter 4, Abu Dhabi: Arab Monetary Fund.

—— (2006) *The Joint Arab Economic Report*, Abu Dhabi: Arab Monetary Fund.

—— (2005) *The Joint Arab Economic Report*, Abu Dhabi: Arab Monetary Fund.

—— (1980) *The Joint Arab Economic Report*, Abu Dhabi: Arab Monetary Fund.

Arab News (2006) 'Remove obstacles to SMEs: Yamani – KSA', *Arab News*, 18 June.

—— (2004a) 'Saud slams neighbors for undermining GCC solidarity', *Arab News*, 6 December.

—— (2004b) 'Saudi Arabia cuts tax rates on foreign investors', *Arab News*, 13 January.

Augustine, B.D. (2007a) 'Gulf is far from currency union', *Gulf News*, 8 September.

—— (2007b) 'Dollar peg at the crossroads', *Gulf News*, 14 November.

Badr-El-Din A.I. (2005) 'Intra-national labor mobility between Arab Gulf Cooperation Council (AGCC) states – towards activating AGCC economic integration process and optimizing human resources exploitation', paper presented at Economic Research Forum, 12th Annual Conference, Cairo, December.

Bahrain Monetary Agency (2007) Statistical Bulletin, August. Available at www.cbb.gov.bh/cmsrule/media/2007/QSB-Aug%202007.pdf (accessed 30 October 2007).

Balassa, B. (1961) *The Theory of Economic Integration*, Homewood, IL: Richard D. Irwin, Inc.

Baldwin, R.E. and Wyplosz, C. (2006) *The Economics of European Integration*, 2nd edn, Maidenhead: McGraw-Hill.

Bank for International Settlements (2005) *International Banking and Financial Market Developments*, BIS Quarterly Review, December.

Barro, R.J. and Gordon, D.B. (1983) 'Rules, discretion and reputation in a model of monetary policy', *Journal of Monetary Economics*, July: 101–121.

Bayoumi, T. and Eichengreen, B. (1997) 'Ever closer to heaven? An optimum-currency-area index for European countries', *European Economic Review*, Vol. 41: 761–770.

—— (1996) 'Is Asia an optimum currency area? Can it become one? Regional, global and historical perspectives on Asian monetary relations', Institute of Business and Economic Research, Center for International and Development Economics Research, Berkeley: University of California.

—— (1992) 'Shocking aspects of European monetary unification', *CEPR Discussion Paper* No. 643, London, May.

—— and Mauro, P. (1999) 'The suitability of ASEAN for a regional currency arrangement', *IMF Working Paper* 162, Washington, DC: International Monetary Fund, December.

BBC News (2007) 'Saudis buy Eurofighters from UK', 17 September.

Bibbo, B. (2005) 'Qatar to build 1b-riyal-facility for small and medium units', *Gulf News*, 6 May.

Bernanke, B. (2004) 'Euro at five: ready for a global role?', paper presented at Institute for International Economics Conference, Washington, DC, 26 February.

Blas, J. and Kerr, S. (2007) 'Gulf consumer spending soars', *Financial Times*, 23 July.

Bley, J. and Chen, K.H. (2006) 'Gulf Cooperation Council (GCC) stock markets: the dawn of a new era', *Global Finance Journal*, Vol. 17: 75–91.

Bolbol, A. and Fatheldin, A.M. (2006) *Foreign and Intra-Arab Capital Flows in the Arab Countries, 1990–2003*, Abu Dhabi: Arab Monetary Fund.

Bosbait, M. and Wilson, R. (2005) 'Education, school to work transitions and unemployment in Saudi Arabia', *Middle Eastern Studies*, Vol. 41, No. 4: 533–545.

Bowman, J. (2007) 'Emirates NBD plans aggressive expansion', *Arabian Business*, 31 October. Available at www.arabianbusiness.com/ (accessed 01 December 2007).

BP (2007) British Petroleum Statistical Review of World Energy, 2007. Available at www.bp.com/productlanding.do?categoryId=91&contentId=7017990) (accessed 23 July 2007).

Bris, A., Koskinen, Y. and Nilsson, M (2002) 'The euro is good after all: corporate evidence', *Working Paper Series in Economics and Finance* No. 510, Stockholm School of Economics, August.

Carvalho, S. (2006) 'GCC investors to pump 1.5b riyals into new Saudi economic city', Dubai: *Gulf News*, 4 July.

—— (2005) 'Dana Gas public offer heading for record oversubscription', *Gulf News*, 25 September.

Cecchini, P. (1988) *The European Challenge 1992: The Benefits of a Single Market*, Aldershot: Wildwood House.

Central Bank of Oman (2000) *25 Years of Central Bank of Oman – April 1975 to April 2000*, Muscat: Central Bank of Oman.

Chami, S., Elekdag, S. and Tchakarov, I. (2004) 'What are the potential economic benefits of enlarging the Gulf Cooperation Council?', *IMF Working Paper* No. 152, Middle East and Central Asia Department, Washington, DC: International Monetary Fund, August.

Chow, H.K. and Kim, Y. (2003a) 'A common currency peg in East Asia? Perspectives from Western Europe', *Journal of Macroeconomics*: 331–350.

—— (2003b) 'Optimum currency area in Europe: an alternative assessment' *Economic Letters*, Vol. 81, No. 3: 297–304.

Commission of the European Communities (1990) 'One market, one money: an evaluation of the potential benefits and costs of forming an economic and monetary union', *European Economy*, No. 44, October.

Cordesman, A.H. (2003) *Saudi Arabia Enters the 21st Century*, Washington, DC: Praeger/Greenwood.

Danthine, J.P., Giavazzi, F. and Ludwig von-Thadden, E. (2000) 'European financial markets after EMU: a first assessment', *NBER Working Paper* No. 8044, Cambridge, MA: National Bureau of Economic Research, December.

Darrat, A.F. and Al-Shamsi, F. (2005) 'On the path of integration in the Gulf region', *Applied Economics*, 37: 1055–1062.

De Grauwe, P. (2007) *Economics of Monetary Union*, 7th edn, Oxford: Oxford University Press.

—— (1993) 'The political economy of monetary union in Europe', *The World Economy*, Vol. 16, No. 6: 653–661.

—— (1975) 'Conditions for monetary integration – a geometric interpretation', *Weltwirtschaftliches Archiv*, Vol. 111, No. 4: 634–646.

Dyer, P. and Yousef, T. (2007) 'Will the current oil boom solve the employment crisis in the Middle East?', *The Arab World Competitiveness Report 2007*, World Economic Forum.

The Economist (2004) 'Arabia's field of dreams', *The Economist*, 27 May.
Egert, B., Ritzberger-Gruenwald, D. and Silgoner, M.A. (2004) 'Inflation differentials in Europe: past experience and future prospects', *Monetary Policy and the Economy*, Austrian Central Bank, May.
EIU (2006a) Economist Intelligence Unit Country Report/Profile for Bahrain, London.
—— (2006b) Economist Intelligence Unit Country Report/Profile for Qatar, London.
—— (1998) Economist Intelligence Unit Oman Country Profile 1997/1998, London.
EIA (2007) 'Energy information administration landed costs of imported crude by area database', US Department of Energy. Available at http://tonto.eia.doe.gov/dnav/pet/pet_pri_top.asp (accessed 10 December 2007).
Eichengreen, B. (1997) 'Is Europe an optimum currency area?', B. Eichengreen, *European Monetary Unification: Theory, Practice, and Analysis*, Cambridge, MA: MIT Press.
—— and Wyplosz, C. (1998) 'Stability pact: more than a minor nuisance?', *Economic Policy*, Vol. 26: 65–113.
Enders, W. and Hurn, S. (1994) 'Theory and tests of generalised purchasing-power parity: common trends and real exchange rates in the Pacific Rim', *Review of International Economics*, Vol. 2, No. 2: 179–190.
Engle, C. and Rogers, J. (1995) 'How wide is the border?', *International Finance Discussion Paper* No. 498, Board of Governors of the Federal Reserve System.
ESCWA (2007) *External Trade Bulletin of the ESCWA Region*, 15th issue, New York: United Nations.
—— (2003) 'Responding to globalization: skill formation and unemployment reduction policies', New York: United Nations.
—— (2001) 'Economic diversification in the oil-producing countries, the case of the Gulf Cooperation Council economics', New York: United Nations, 10 January.
Esquivel, G. and Larrain, F.B, (2002) 'The impact of G-3 exchange rate volatility on developing countries', *G24 Discussion Paper Series* No. 16, New York and Geneva: United Nations, January.
Evans-Pritchard, A. (2006) 'Trillion dollar gamble on future of Gulf', *The Daily Telegraph*, 9 May.
Executive Magazine (2007) 'UAE, Oman link exchanges', February, No. 91. Available at www.executive-magazine.com/91/article.php?id=934 (accessed 1 December 2007).
Fasano, U. (2000) 'Review of the experience with oil stabilization and savings funds in selected countries', *IMF Working Paper* No. 112, Washington, DC: International Monetary Fund.
—— and Goyal, R. (2004) 'Emerging strains in GCC labour markets', *IMF Working Paper* No. 71, Washington, DC: International Monetary Fund.
—— and Staff Team (2003) 'Monetary union among member countries of the Gulf Cooperation Council', Washington, DC: International Monetary Fund.
—— and Wang, Q. (2002) 'Testing the relationship between government spending and revenue: evidence from GCC countries', *IMF Working Paper* No. 201, Washington, DC: International Monetary Fund.
Feldstein, M. (1997) 'The political economy of the European economic and monetary union: political sources of an economic liability', *Journal of Economic Perspectives*, Vol. 11, No. 4: 23–42.
Fielding, D. and Shields, K. (2005) 'The impact of monetary union on macroeconomic integration: evidence from West Africa', *Economica*, Vol. 72: 683–704.
Frankel, J.A. (2003) 'A proposed monetary regime for small commodity exporters: peg to the export price (PEP)', *International Finance*, Vol. 6, No. 1: 61–88.

—— and Rose, A.K. (2000) 'Estimating the effect of currency unions on trade and output', *NBER Working Paper* No. 7857, Cambridge, MA: National Bureau of Economic Research.
—— (1997) 'Is EMU more justifiable ex post than ex ante?' *European Economic Review*, Vol. 41: 753–760.
—— (1996) 'The endogeneity of the optimum currency area criteria', *NBER Working Paper* No. 5700, Cambridge, MA: National Bureau of Economic Research.
Galati, G. and Tsatsaronis, K. (2001) 'The impact of the euro on Europe's financial markets', *Bank for International Settlements Working Paper* No. 100, July.
GCC Secretariat General (2006) *GCC Achievements in Figures 2006*, Riyadh: GCC Secretariat General. Available at www.gcc-sg.org/ (accessed 1 October 2007).
—— (2001) *The Economic Agreement*, Riyadh: GCC Secretariat General, 31 December. Available at www.gcc-sg.org (accessed 20 October 2006).
—— (1981) *Unified Economic Agreement*, Riyadh: GCC Secretariat General. Available at www.gcc-sg.org (accessed 20 October 2006).
Ghars El-Din, M.A.H. and Mohammad, Y.H.J. (2005) 'Exchange rate and domestic prices in the GCC countries', *Economic Research Forum Working Paper* No. 0105, Egypt, January.
Ghosh, A.R., Gulde, A.M., Ostry, J.D. and Wolf, H.C. (1997) 'Does the nominal exchange rate regime matter?' *NBER Working Paper Series* No. 5874, Cambridge, MA: National Bureau of Economic Research, January.
Girgis, M. (2002) 'The GCC factor in future Arab labour migration', paper presented at Fourth Mediterranean Development Forum, Amman, October.
—— (2000) 'National versus migrant workers in the GCC: coping with change', paper presented at Mediterranean Development Forum Labor Workshop, Cairo, 5–8 March.
Glavan, B. (2004) 'The failure of OCA analysis', *Quarterly Journal of Austrian Economics*, Vol. 7, No. 2, June.
Grubel, H. (2005) 'Small country benefits from monetary union', *Journal of Policy Modeling*, Vol. 27: 509–523.
—— and Lloyd, P.J. (1975) *Intra-Industry Trade: The Theory and Measurement of International Trade in Differentiated Products*, New York: Wiley.
Gulf Daily News (2006) 'Saudi to privatise bourse', *Gulf Daily News*, 10 May.
Gulf News (2007a) 'No dollar announcement at GCC summit', *Gulf News*, 4 December 2007.
—— (2007b) 'GCC monetary union deadline difficult to meet', *Gulf News*, 9 September.
—— (2006) 'UAE becomes top investor in Saudi Arabia', *Gulf News*, 18 June.
Gulf Research Center (2005a) *GCC Economic Report*, Issue 3, Dubai, October 2005.
—— (2005b) *GCC Economic Report*, Issue 5, Dubai, December 2005.
Gulf Times (2007) 'GCC may set up currency board to manage union', *Gulf Times*, 24 February.
—— (2004) 'Volatile oil is a headache for Gulf monetary union', *Gulf Times*, 30 October.
Hammoudeh, S. and Kyongwook C. (2004) 'Volatility regime-switching and linkage among GCC stock markets', *Economic Research Forum*, Egypt, December.
Hassanain, K. (2004) 'Price convergence and the GCC monetary union', *Journal of International Business and Economics*, Vol. 1: 12–17.
Husain, S. (2007) 'Currency union date "in doubt" ', *Gulf News*, 23 December.
Healy, C. (2003) 'EMU: lessons for the CFA zone', paper presented at 8th European Union Studies Association (EUSA) Biennial Conference, Nashville, 27–29 March.

Holden, D. and Johns, R. (1981) *The House of Saud*, London: Sidgwick & Jackson.
Hoyos, C. and Khalaf, R. (2006) 'Saudi Arabia upsets UAE pipeline plans', *Financial Times*, 11 July.
Humayon, A. and Presley, J.R. (2001) *The Gulf Co-operation Council: A Slow Path to Integration?* London: Blackwell.
IIF (Institute of International Finance) (2007) 'Capital flows to emerging market economies', London, 31 May. Available at www.iif.com/press/press+44.php (accessed 8 December 2007).
IEA (2007) International Energy Agency, Energy Prices and Taxes database.
IMF (2007a) World Economic Outlook Database, October.
—— (2007b) Direction of Trade Statistics Database, October.
—— (2007c) World Economic and Financial Surveys, *Regional Economic Outlook: Middle East and Central Asia*, Washington, DC: International Monetary Fund, October.
—— (2007d) International Financial Statistics Database, October.
—— (2007e) 'Eastern Caribbean currency union: 2006 regional discussions – staff report', *Country Report* No. 07/96, Washington, DC: International Monetary Fund.
—— (2007f) United Arab Emirates: 2007 Article IV Consultation, No. 07/347, Washington, DC: International Monetary Fund.
—— (2006a) United Arab Emirates: 2006 Article IV Consultation, No. 06/257, Washington, DC: International Monetary Fund.
—— (2006b) World Economic and Financial Surveys, *Regional Economic Outlook: Middle East and Central Asia*, Washington, DC: International Monetary Fund, May.
—— (2005a) United Arab Emirates: 2005 Article IV Consultation – Staff Report, *County Report* No. 05/269, Washington, DC: International Monetary Fund.
—— (2005b) World Economic and Financial Surveys, *Regional Economic Outlook: Middle East and Central Asia*, Washington, DC: International Monetary Fund, September.
—— (1996) 'Policy challenges in the Gulf Cooperation Council countries', Middle Eastern Department, May, Washington, DC: International Monetary Fund.
Issa, N. (2006) 'Integration of GCC stock markets: to cross list or not to cross list?', *Arab Press Digest*, 18 January.
Issing, O. (2004) 'The ECB and the euro: the first five years', London: Institute of Economic Affairs, *Occasional Paper* No. 134.
Jadresic, E. (2002) 'On a common currency for the GCC countries', *IMF Policy Discussion Paper*, Washington, DC: International Monetary Fund, December.
Johri, D. and Miller, M. (2002) 'Devaluation of the rupee: tale of two years, 1966 and 1991', *CCS Working Paper* No. 0028, New Delhi: Centre for Civil Society. Available at www.ccsindia.org/ccsindia/policy/money/studies/wp0028.pdf (accessed 29 December 2007).
Kamar, B. and Ben Naceur, S. (2007) 'GCC monetary union and the degree of macroeconomic policy coordination', *IMF Working Paper* No. 249, Washington, DC: International Monetary Fund, October.
Kaufmann, D., Kraay, A. and Mastruzzi, M. (2007) 'Governance matters VI: governance indicators for 1996–2006', *World Bank Policy Research Working Paper* No. 4280. Available at http://ssrn.com/ (accessed 9 November 2007).
Kenen, P.B. (1969) 'The theory of optimum currency areas: an eclectic view', in R.A. Mundell and A.K. Swoboda (eds) *Monetary Problems of the International Economy*, Chicago: University of Chicago Press.
Kerr, S. (2007a) 'Gulf aims to make tenth of global output', *Financial Times*, 9 October.

—— (2007b) 'Emirate sets its sights on trebled GDP by 2015', *Financial Times*, 24 July.

Khalaf, R. (2006) 'UAE shifts 10% of its reserves into euros', *Financial Times*, 13 July.

—— (2002) 'Saudi Arabia urged to speed up economic reform', *Financial Times*, 23 October.

Khaleej Times (2006) 'IMF calls for official data on inflation', *Khaleej Times*, 19 December.

—— (2004) 'UAE set to host AGCC central bank: Kuwait', *Khaleej Times*, 25 October.

King, R. and Levine, R. (1993) 'Finance and growth: Schumpeter might be right', *Quarterly Journal of Economics*, Vol. 108: 717–725.

Kingdom of Saudi Arabia (2000) 'Socio-economic developments during the sixth plan: chapter two of the seventh development plan', Ministry of Economy and Planning. Available at http://http://www.planning.gov.sa/ (accessed 7 October 2007).

KPMG (1998) 'Europe's Preparedness for EMU', *Research Report 1998*, Brussels/London: KPMG Management Consulting.

Krueger, R. and Kovarich, E. (2006) 'Some principles for development of statistics for a Gulf Cooperation Council currency union', *IMF Working Paper* No. 38, Washington, DC: International Monetary Fund, June.

Krugman, P. (1993) 'Lessons of Massachusetts for EMU', in F. Giavazzi and F. Torres (eds) *The Transition to Economic and Monetary Union in Europe*, New York: Cambridge University Press.

Kumar, P.A. (2006) 'Central Bank of Oman defends fixed peg of rial to dollar', *Times of Oman*, 16 May.

Laabas, B. and Limam, I. (2002) 'Are GCC countries ready for currency union?', Kuwait: Arab Planning Institute, April.

Leblond, P. (2004) 'Completing the Maastricht contract: institutional handicraft and the transition to European Monetary Union', *Journal of Common Market Studies*, Vol. 42, No. 3: 553–572.

Legrenzi, M. (2002) 'The Gulf Cooperation Council in light of international relations theory', *International Area Review*, Vol. 5, No. 2, Autumn.

Liquidity Management Centre (2007) Global sukuk table. Available at www.lmcbahrain.com/Global-table.asp (accessed 29 November 2007).

Looney, R.E. (2004) 'Saudization and sound economic reforms: are the two compatible?', Center for Contemporary Conflict, *Strategic Insights*, Vol. III, No. 2.

—— (2003) 'Economic integration in the Gulf region: does the future hold more promise than the past,? Center for Contemporary Conflict, *Strategic Insight*, Vol. II, No. 3..

—— (2001) 'Saudi Arabia: measures of transition from a rentier state', in J. Kechichian (ed.) *Iran, Iraq and the Arab Gulf States*, New York: Palgrave.

Lucas, R. (1976) 'Econometric policy evaluation: a critique', in K. Brunner and A. Meltzer (eds) 'The Phillips curve and labor markets', *Carnegie-Rochester Conference Series on Public Policy* No. 1: 19–46.

Luciani, G. (2007) 'The GCC refining and petrochemical sectors in global perspective', in E. Woertz (ed.) *Gulf Geo-Economics*, Dubai: Gulf Research Center.

—— (2006) 'The pace and problems with GCC privatizations', *Gulf Yearbook 2005–2006*, Dubai: Gulf Research Center.

—— and Beblawi, H. (1987) *The Rentier State*, London: Croom Helm.

Mattli, W. (1999) *The Logic of Regional Integration: Europe and Beyond*, New York: Cambridge University Press.

McKinnon, R.I. (1963) 'Optimum currency areas', *American Economic Review*, Vol. 53, No. 4: 717–725.

McSheehy, W. (2006) 'Investors set up market to handle Islamic bonds', *International Herald Tribune*, 7 June.

MENA Report (2006) 'GCC IPO market to soar over the next two years', 26 February. Available at www.menareport.com/en/business,Financial_Markets/195124 (accessed 10 October 2007).

Middle East Economic Digest (2006) 'Emaar unveils King Abdullah Economic City', 6 January. Available at www.meed.com (accessed 10 December 2007).

Middle East Economic Survey (2005) 'GCC summit', *Middle East Economic Survey*, Vol. 48, 52, 26 December. Available at www.mees.com/postedarticles/oped/v48n52–5OD02.htm (accessed 30 November 2007).

Mohammad, Y.H.J. and El-Sakka, M.I.T (2001) 'Demand for imports in the GCC countries', *Journal of the Gulf and Arabian Peninsula Studies*, Vol. 27, No. 100: 43–84.

Mundell, R. A (1997) 'Updating the agenda for monetary union', in M.I. Blejer, J.A. Frenkel, Leiderman, L. and Razin, A. (eds) *Optimum Currency Areas: New Analytical and Policy Developments*, Washington, DC: International Monetary Fund.

—— (1973) 'Uncommon arguments for common currencies', in H.G. Johnson and A.K. Swoboda (eds) *The Economics of Common Currencies*, Cambridge: Harvard University Press.

—— (1961) 'A theory of optimum currency areas', *American Economic Review*, Vol. 51, No. 4: 657–665.

National Bank of Kuwait (2007) 'GCC banking – special review', Kuwait, May. Available at www.nbk.com/NR/rdonlyres/33044F9F-8324–454D-B883–92CB28AF915D/0/NBK_Review_GCCBanking_0705.pdf (accessed 12 December 2007).

Nitsch, V. (2005) 'Have a break, have a national currency: when do monetary unions fall apart?', in P. De Grauwe and J. Melitz (eds) *Prospects for Monetary Unions After the Euro*, Cambridge, MA: MIT Press.

OPEC (2006) 'Annual statistical bulletin: 2006', Vienna: Organisation of the Petroleum Exporting Countries.

The Peninsula (2006) 'Saudi has no plan to revalue riyal: official', *The Peninsula*, 26 June.

Qasrawi, S. (2004) 'Foreign direct investment in the UAE: determinants and recommendations', Abu Dhabi: Emirates Center for Strategic Studies and Research, Occasional Papers series.

Rana, P.B. (2007) 'Economic integration and synchronization of business cycles in East Asia', *Journal of Asian Economics*, Vol. 18: 711–725.

Reuters News Agency (2007) 'Saudi Arabia to cut government spending', Reuters, 9 May.

—— (2004) 'Saudi mobile phone IPO 50 times oversubscribed', Reuters, 31 October.

Robinson, A. and Morse, E. (2007) 'Saudi Arabia may hold key to oil and dollar link', *Financial Times*, 24 October.

Rogers, J.A. (2002) 'Monetary union, price level convergence, and inflation: how close is Europe to the United States?', *International Finance Discussion Paper* No. 740, Board of Governors of the Federal Reserve System, October.

Rose, A.K. (1999) 'One money, one market, estimating the effect of common currencies on trade', *NBER Working Paper* No. 7432, Cambridge, MA: National Bureau of Economic Research, December.

Ross, M.L. (1999) 'The political economy of the resource curse, *World Politics*, Vol. 51, No. 2: 297–322.

Rutledge, E. (2008a) 'Is EMU a viable model for monetary integration in the Arabian Gulf?' *The Journal of Economic Policy Reform*, vol. II, issue 2, June.

—— (2008a) 'Business expectations for a common currency in the Arabian Gulf', *Journal of Development and Economic Policies*, Vol. 10, No. 1, January.

—— (2007) *A Gulf Cooperation Council Currency Union: Appropriateness and Implications*, unpublished thesis, University of Durham.

—— (2006a) 'GCC economic performance in 2005', *Gulf Yearbook 2005–2006*, Dubai: Gulf Research Center.

—— (2006b) 'Value-added across the board', *Gulf in the Media Business Bulletin*, Dubai: Gulf Research Center.

Sajini, I. (2004) 'Effects of WTO on small & medium enterprises', *Arab News*, 19 January.

SAMA (2007) Monthly statistical bulletin, July. Available at www.sama.gov.sa/bulletins_files/monthly/monthly_bulletin.pdf (accessed 1 December 2007).

Sassanpour, C., Joharhi, G. Kireyev, A. and Petri, M. (1997) 'Labour market challenges and policies in the Gulf Cooperation Council countries', Washington, DC: International Monetary Fund.

Sender, H., Wighton, D. and Tucker, S. (2007) 'Saudis plan huge sovereign wealth fund', *Financial Times*, 21 December.

Setser, B. (2007) 'Oil and global adjustment', Washington, DC: Peterson Institute for International Economics. Available at: www.iie.com/publications/pb/pb07–4/setser.pdf (accessed 2 November 2007).

Shah, N.M. (2005) 'Restrictive labour immigration policies in the oil-rich Gulf: effectiveness and implications for sending Asian countries', paper presented at United Nations Expert Group Meeting on International Migration and Development in the Arab Region, Beirut, May 2006.

Shirian, D. (2006) 'Yemen is a Gulf state',: *Al-Hayat*, 7 June.

Soltwedel, R., Dohse, D. and Krieger-Boden, C. (1999) 'EMU challenges European labour markets', *IMF Working Paper* No. 131, Washington, DC: International Monetary Fund.

Sturm, M. and Siegfried, N. (2005) 'Regional monetary integration in the member states of the Gulf Cooperation Council', *Occasional Paper Series* No. 31, Frankfurt: European Central Bank, June.

UAE Interact (2006) *UAE Yearbook 2006*, National Media Council, UAE. Available at www.uaeinteract.com/uaeint_misc/pdf_2005/index.asp (accessed 18 September 2007).

UNCTAD (2007) *World Investment Report*, 2007. Available at www.unctad.org/fdistatistics (accessed 10 October 2007).

UNDP (2007) 'Programme on governance in the Arab region, financial management': Qatar. Available at www.pogar.org/countries/finances.asp?cid=15.

UN (2006) *Commodity Trade Statistics Database.* Available at: http://comtrade.un.org/db/ (accessed 18 November 2007).

—— (2004) *Arab Human Development Report 2004*, New York: United Nations Development Programme.

—— (2002) *Arab Human Development Report 2002*, New York: United Nations Development Programme.

Wallis, W. (2005) 'Tourism: growing appeal leaves observers baffled', *Financial Times*, 12 July.

Willett, T.D. (2000) 'Some political economy aspects of EMU', *Journal of Policy Modeling*, Vol. 22, No. 3: 379–389.

Wilson, R.J.A. (2004) 'Exchange rate issues for Muslim economies', paper presented at International Seminar on Macroeconomics in Islamic Perspective, International Islamic University, Malaysia, September.

World Bank (2007a) World Development Indicators database, June.
—— (2007b) *Doing Business 2007* Available at www.doingbusiness.org/ExploreEconomies/?economyid=74 (accessed 12 April 2007).
—— (2006) *Economic Developments and Prospects: Financial Markets in a New Age of Oil*, Middle East and North Africa Region, Washington, DC: World Bank.
Zafar, A. (2004) 'The rentier state in Gabon', *World Bank Policy Research Working Paper* No. 3403, Washington, DC: The World Bank.

Index